CHILDREN OF POVERTY

STUDIES ON THE EFFECTS OF SINGLE PARENTHOOD, THE FEMINIZATION OF POVERTY, AND HOMELESSNESS

edited by

STUART BRUCHEY
UNIVERSITY OF MAINE

A GARLAND SERIES

"NOT JUST A SHELTER KID"

How Homeless Children Find Solace

MELANIE SMITH PERCY

GARLAND PUBLISHING, INC.
NEW YORK & LONDON / 1997

Library of Congress Cataloging-in-Publication Data

Percy, Melanie Smith, 1955–
    Not just a shelter kid : how homeless children find solace /
Melanie Smith Percy.
        p.   cm. — (Children of poverty)
    Includes bibliographical references and index.
    ISBN 0-8153-2618-1 (alk. paper)
    1. Homeless children—United States—Attitudes. 2. Home-
less children—United States—Psychology. 3. Shelters for the
homeless—United States. I. Title. II. Series.
HV4505.P47 1997
362.7'086'942—dc21   96-30013

Printed on acid-free, 250-year-life paper
Manufactured in the United States of America

Contents

List of Tables

Acknowledgments

My deepest thanks to Dr. Pamela N. Clarke for her patient determination, encouragement and insistence that my doctoral studies and dissertation research were sustained at the highest level of intellectual ability. Also, for her considerable commitment of time and energy to this project. I am indebted to my committee members Drs. Carol E. Davis, Sandra B. Frick-Helms, and Julie Neureur for their enthusiastic insights, critical reflection and their unfailing support throughout this process, specifically to Dr. Neureur for her inspirational teaching, to Dr. Davis for her expertise in qualitative data analysis and for always being there, and to Dr. Frick-Helms for sharing herself, her understanding and her love of children.

I would like to thank the child-participants who so willingly and enthusiastically shared their work, their ideas and themselves.

I am grateful to my colleague and close friend, Judy Corfman, RN, FNP for her seemingly inexhaustible encouragement and support at exactly the right moments, including the best ever chocolate chip cookies. Also, to Cheryl Prickett, RN, PNP for assistance in analyzing the data and her boundless enthusiasm for this project. This book would not be complete without adding my sincere thanks and gratitude to Sue Walker and Elena Mota for their very patient and painstaking retyping of this manuscript.

I would like to thank the faculty of the School of Nursing, University of South Carolina for the freedom to create and explore new paths throughout the doctoral program.

Finally, I will be forever indebted to my husband Tomm for his strength, loving understanding, and sustaining belief that I would complete this project. Also, for insisting that I learn to use the computer and for providing computer support without complaint at three a.m., or whenever I needed him. I would like to thank our three children (Ian, Laura and Kayla) for generously giving up time with their mother so she could fulfill her dream. Watching them grow, listening to their ideas and re-experiencing childhood through their eyes has fueled my interest and understanding of what is special to children.

Preface

This book is about children, and their perspectives. These children were homeless at the time of these interviews. However, their questions, thoughts, and feelings are not unique to homeless children. The many issues of childhood remain the same regardless of where the child lives. The ideas expressed in these pages are some of the universal themes of growing up and becoming an adult. Their search for identity, the desire to care for someone and have them care for you, trust, stability in an ever-changing world. All of these themes were present in the children's interviews and photographs.

The children were intensely involved in this project. They were very serious about their assignment from the time they spent with the camera, throughout the interviews. Their thoughts are presented here in the hopes that the reader will take away a more complete understanding of what it means to be a child living in a shelter.

Melanie S. Percy
Austin, Texas

"Not Just a Shelter Kid"

I

No Where To Go, No Place To Be

Over 2.2 million people are homeless in the United States, more than at any time since the Great Depression.[1] The number of Americans living on the street or in shelters increases yearly by about 25%.[2] Approximately one third of this population is comprised of families, generally headed by women with two to three children.[3] These vulnerable children number between 100,000 and 750,000 and their ranks are increasing daily.[4] Indeed, families with children are the fastest-growing segment of the homeless population.[5]

Increasing poverty, coupled with a lack of affordable housing, has driven many families into the streets. Between 1981 and 1985, the number of American families living in poverty increased by more than 40%.[6] According to the US Bureau of Census almost 45% of African-American children, and 39% of Spanish-American children are living below the poverty line.[7] The average wait for public housing in most major cities is two years. In some cities the waiting lists became so long they were officially closed.[8] Several factors have been identified which have contributed to the shortage of affordable housing: the gentrification of neighborhoods, the freeze on welfare shelter allowances and the Regan/Buash Administration's decision to curtail spending on low income housing.[9] The decision to reduce government funding for the most vulnerable populations has led to the current epidemic of homelessness in the United States.

Homeless children face tremendous challenges. Bassuk and Rubin found severe anxiety and depression among homeless children in Massachusetts.[10] According to Davidhizar and Frank, 50% of homeless children between the ages of seven and eleven years have scores on a depression scale that indicate a need for further evaluation.[11] Additionally, an increased incidence of family violence and child abuse or neglect has been documented in these families.[12]

Rafferty and Shinn, and Wright found evidence of increased reports of acute and chronic illness among homeless children.[13] Murata, et al. found few chronic health problems among homeless children, but a high prevalence of otitis media, pharyngitis and accidental injury and a high incidence of immunization delays.[14] Schulsinger identified a lack of preventive health care, poor nutrition, and difficulty attending school among children residing in shelters.[15]

Obtaining access to government programs may be problematic when a family is residing in a shelter. Establishing eligibility for government programs is difficult when families do not have a permanent address. Homeless shelters do not generally allow their occupants to use the shelter's address on applications. In some shelters, there is no refrigeration so mothers cannot use the free milk given to them by the Women, Infant, Children (WIC) food supplement program.[16]

Daily routines, which are commonplace for most American children, present difficulties for homeless children. Homelessness does not always mean unemployment for parents, yet parents are often forced to choose between keeping their job or escorting their children through unsafe neighborhoods to unfamiliar schools. Caring for preschool children is problematic for homeless parents, especially when shelter regulations require them to search daily for permanent housing. Few shelters have play space for children, and many are in neighborhoods where there is no room for outside play.

Depression, anxiety and learning difficulties are common among these school-age children, poor school attendance and truancy are also problems. The National Committee for the Homeless estimates that 57% of homeless school-age children do not regularly attend school.[17] Less than 40% of children between the ages of ten and sixteen at the Martinique Hotel (the largest welfare hotel in New York City) attend school. Whitman, Accardo, and Kendagor assert that schools should provide the stable, supportive emotional environment that homeless children need.[18] Instead, schools are part of the problem. Teachers and peers often label and stereotype homeless children, resulting in their further isolation.[19]

The majority of the studies on homeless families have focused on family dysfunction or the stress and problems encountered in homelessness. While necessary, the problem-focused approach of these research studies provides a very narrow, limited understanding of the experience of homelessness for children. There is a danger inherent in identifying problems within this population without also identifying strengths. The love and loyalty seen within many homeless families is nothing short of heroic.[20] Focusing only on the problems, without a concomitant focus on the bureaucracy which allows these situations to continue, risks labeling the homeless as defective and subhuman. At present, the United States has a more efficient and humane system for dealing with stray animals than with people who are homeless.[21]

THE TRAUMA OF DISPOSSESSION

Goodman, Saxe, and Harvey characterize homelessness as psychological trauma.[22] Either the gradual or sudden loss of stable housing produces symptoms of trauma. "The essence of trauma is the perceived severance of affiliative bonds which damages the psychological sense of trust, safety and security."[23] Individuals who are traumatized by homelessness lose faith in their ability to care for themselves and in the willingness of others to help them. They often develop a distrust of others.[24] They are in reality the dispossessed: "without property or status, displaced persons, having suffered the loss of expectations, prospects, relationships; disinherited, disaffiliated, alienated."[25] Children may suffer the most from the effects of shelter life.[26]

Current literature suggests that shelter life is traumatic for children. Investigators have primarily used psychometric measures to examine depression, anxiety, and developmental delays in children residing in public shelters.[27] Few researchers have interviewed homeless adults or children in an attempt to understand the experience of homelessness.[28] No studies have examined the impact of family bonds, hope, or the meaning of life for these children. In order to fully understand the experience of being homeless, it is necessary to obtain a more complete picture of the lives of children residing in shelters.

CONDUCTING RESEARCH WITH CHILDREN

Conventional research methods have limited applicability for children. Language differences between children and adults make it difficult to interview preschool and school-age children. Researchers frequently assume they understand the child's frame of reference, although the child and adult differ widely in terms of life experience and maturation.[29] Quantitative testing methods are equally problematic as children become distracted and bored by testing situations. Their desire to please the adult researcher may also interfere with data collection.[30] The difficulties of conducting research with children has led many researchers to use adult informants to interpret the meaning of the child's experience, though even parents and caretakers may misinterpret a child's understandings.[31]

Research Question

The central question guiding this research was: How do homeless children portray and describe what is special to them? Moustakas' heuristic method was adapted to include photographic data.[32] This study used the children's own photography to systematically determine what was special to them.

The limitations of conventional study designs and the paucity of data available on homeless children required a unique approach to the research question. The specifications of this study were to:

> 1) Explicate what was special to homeless children as portrayed by their photographs and their descriptions of their photographs.
>
> 2) Determine the feasibility of using photography as a data generating technique with school-age children.

In this study, the researcher focused on illuminating the child's perspective. Children used photography to portray and describe what was special to them.

Terms

Throughout this study the terms *homeless, family, school-age child, describe photography,* and *special* were repeatedly used. These orienting terms are defined below in order to clarify their meaning in this study.

The literature provides no clear definition of *homeless*. In the broadest sense and as used in this study, homeless was defined as "those who do not have regular or customary access to a continual dwelling or residence."[33] For the purposes of this study homeless children were additionally defined as children of families residing in a shelter designated for the homeless.

A *family* is defined as at least one adult over the age of seventeen and one child under the age of seventeen. This definition is currently used by the family shelter where this study was conducted.

A *school-age child* is a child between the ages of 6 and 12 years.

The term *describes photography* relates to the children's verbal interpretations of their photographs. In a heuristic study, the most valuable element is the nature and meaning of experiences. Photography was the medium used to capture the child's view, while the description of the photographs gave the researcher a glimpse of the child's meanings.

The term *special* is defined in *The Random House Dictionary of the English Language* as something "extraordinary; as in amount or degree."[34] For the purpose of this study the child-participants and researcher defined *special* as "something that is really close to you that you love deeply or care about" (discussed in further detail in Chapter 3).

ORIENTING FRAMEWORK

Identification with a nursing theory informs and illuminates practice and the emergence of research questions. Jean Watson's conceptualization of Human Care was the orienting framework used in the development and construction of this study. The research question and the research method chosen evolved directly from the investigator's interest in caring and the meaning of experience.

Human Care

Caring is more than an emotion or concern. Caring as a moral ideal "involves values, a will, a commitment to care, knowledge, caring actions and consequences."[35] Caring involves a commitment to the protection, enhancement, and preservation of the dignity of women, men and children.[36] It is embedded in understanding meanings and the subjective human response to experience.

Watson has proposed ten carative factors which give a framework to caring. These carative factors guide the nurse in the development of a relationship between the nurse and the client. Watson terms this relationship the human care process, when the nurse co-participates in gaining control, becoming knowledgeable and promoting health changes.[37] The carative factors include:

1. Humanistic-altruistic system of values.
2. Faith-hope.
3. Sensitivity to self and others.
4. Helping-trusting, human care relationship.
5. Expressing positive and negative feelings.
6. Creative problem-solving caring process.
7. Transpersonal teaching-learning.
8. Supportive, protective and/or corrective mental, physical, societal, and spiritual environment.

9. Human needs assistance.
10. Existential-phenomenological-spiritual
    forces.[38]

Nursing care guided by these carative factors will lead to an affirmation of human care as an intersubjective transpersonal human process. The carative factors become actualized in the moment-to-moment human care process in which the nurse is "being with the other person." According to Watson, health is the unity of and harmony within the mind, body and soul. Humans possess unique inner resources and strengths that can be drawn upon to meet health challenges. Human health goals can be met through "finding meaning in one's existence, discovering inner power and control, and potentiating instances of transcendence and self-healing."[39] The goal of nursing is to "help persons gain a higher degree of harmony within the mind, body and soul which generates self-knowledge, self-reverence, self-healing, and self-care processes while allowing increasing diversity."[40]

Watson's conceptualization of Human Care explicates Carl Rogers' concepts of authenticity and self-direction in regards to the nurse-client relationship. Watson defines authenticity as transpersonal caring where each person is touched by the human center of the other.[41]

In this moment lies the potential for mutuality, a heightened sensitivity to the self and others. Humans are interconnected within the universe, therefore the pursuit of caring knowledge is viewed within the framework of "shared humaneness."[42] The participation of the nurse in the lived reality of the other person is possible only where caring, compassion and concern exist. The one who is cared for can then release feeling and thoughts which had not been expressed. When the nurse and client are co-participants in caring, self-healing and harmony are released in both. Time, space and self are transcended through an interconnectedness.[43] Through caring, compassion and concern the individual may reveal the meanings they assign to their experience.

Play Therapy

Research questions formed within Jean Watson's conceptualization of Human Care can be explored through qualitative methods. Qualitative methods are uniquely suited to the development of research programs designed to describe and interpret human experience when the meaning of the experience for the individual is of paramount importance.[44] Manicus and Secord agree that "to understand a person we must grasp the person's meanings and understandings, motivations and intentions."[45] When children are the research participants it is important to use a research method which can navigate the complexities inherent in conducting research with children. This is a difficult task because expressive language skills develop at different ages. Children may be reluctant to speak with adults, or they may have a limited vocabulary and cannot fully express their ideas. For these reasons an alternative to the conventional interview method must be developed when children's meanings and understandings are the research focus.

The methods of client-centered play can be adapted to form research avenues for child-participants. Client-centered non-directive play therapy techniques were developed by Virginia Axline, from the teachings of Carl Rogers.[46] Play is the child's natural medium of self-expression.[47] During play a child explores, constructs, understands and assimilates the world. The content, theme, and process of spontaneous play provide information about the child's thoughts, beliefs and feelings.[48] The basic philosophy of Axline's approach acknowledges the ability of individuals to express and solve their own problems. The therapist creates an accepting, non-threatening environment enabling the child to freely experience an inner world, and activate self-curative powers in the unique development of the self.[49] The child's self-growth, self-direction and self-exploration develop as the therapist uses empathic reflecting to demonstrate total acceptance. A non-threatening environment which enables children to freely experience their inner world encourages the expressions of meaning and values. The genuineness or authenticity of the therapist's interaction with the client is crucial to the development of the therapeutic relationship.[50]

SIGNIFICANCE OF THE STUDY

This study was vital because of (a) the rapidly increasing number of homeless families; (b) research documenting the detrimental effects of homelessness on children's health and development and; (c) the limited number of studies exploring the child's perspective of the world. Increases in the numbers of homeless families means that more and more children are exposed to the challenges of homelessness.

Children's perceptions of the changes in their lives have been largely unexplored. It is imperative to achieve an understanding of the total experience of homelessness before interventions and programs are planned. In Berck's book *No Place to Be: Voices of Homeless Children*, Kareem, age 14, poignantly describes shelter life:

> The shelter is only another home, it's
> not another life. It's not like I just
> moved into another life like an alien
> . . . the shelter doesn't control who
> you are. Don't let it be that you're a
> 'shelter kid', let it be that you're a kid
> in a shelter.[51]

This quote from a 14 year-old-boy living in a shelter emphasizes the necessity of viewing the homeless not as a damaged population, but as individuals reacting to life in extraordinary circumstances. This study is vital to nursing because it broadens the current knowledge of the experience of homeless children. These children are experiencing a phenomena which is new to modern America. There are no precedents for dealing with the magnitude of today's homeless population. At present, the impact of homelessness on the future physical and emotional health of children is undetermined. The holistic focus of nursing places the discipline in an ideal position to address the needs of this very vulnerable population.

Effective nursing practice must be grounded in theory developed through research. The need for theory directed practice must continue to be stressed and demonstrated in nursing education. Only then can nursing comprehensively address the needs of the community. Qualitative research methods give voice to individual needs, desires and outlooks. In order to care more adequately for people, a deeper understanding of their perspective is necessary. According to Watson, "human caring must be concerned with the meaning of being and not reduce humans ways of being to only human knowing and doing."[52]

NOTES

1. Bassuk, E.L., & Rosenberg, L. (1988). "Why does family homelessness occur? A case-control study." *American Journal of Public Health*, 78(7), 783-788.

2. Foscarinis, M. (1991). "The politics of homelessness." *American Psychologist*, 46(11), 1232-1238.

3. Bassuk, E. & Rubin, L. (1987). "Homeless hildren: A neglected population." *American Journal of Orthopsychiatry*, 57(2), 279-286; Rossi, P.H. (1989). *Down and Out in America*. Chicago: University of Chicago Press; Schulsinger, E. (1990). "Needs of sheltered homeless children." *Journal of Pediatric Health Care*, 4(3), 136-140; Wright, J.D. (1991). "Children in and of the streets: Health, social policy and the homeless young." *American Journal of Diseases of Children*, 145, 516-519.

4. Schulsinger, see note 3 above.

5. Wood, D. (1989). "Homeless children: Their evaluation and treatment." *Journal of Pediatric Health Care*, 3(4), 194-199.

6. Wood, D. (1992). "Evaluation and management of homeless families and children." In D. Wood (Ed.), *Delivering Health Care to Homeless Persons*, NY, NY: Springer Publishing.

7. Murata, J., Mace, J.P., Streholow, A. & Shuler, P. (1992). "Disease patterns in homeless children: A comparison with national data." *Journal of Pediatric Nursing*, 7(3), 196-203.

8. Foscarinis, see note 2 above.

9. Berne, A.S., Dato, C., Mason, D.J., & Fafferty, M. (1990). "A nursing model for addressing the health needs of homeless families." *Image*, 22(1), 8-13.

10. Bassuk & Rubin, see note 3 above.

11. Davidhizer, R., & Frank, B. (1992). "Understanding the physical and psychosocial stressors of the child who is homeless." *Pediatric Nursing*, 18(6), 559-562.

12. Bassuk & Rosenberg, see note 1 above; Molnar, J., Rath, W., & Klein, T. (1990). "Constantly compromised: The impact of homelessness on children." *Journal of Social Issues*, 46(4), 109-123; Wood, see note 6 above.

13. Rafferty, & Y. & Shinn, M. (1991). "The impact of homelessness on children." *American Psychologist*, 46(11), 1170-1179; Wright, see note 3 above.

14. Murata, et al., see note 7 above.

15. Schulsinger, see note 3 above.

16. Schulsinger, see note 3 above.

17. Rafferty & Shinn, see note 13 above.

18. Whitman, B.Y., Accardo, P., Boyert, M., & Kendagor, R. (1990). "Homelessness and cognitive performance in children: A possible link." *Social Work*, 35(6), 516-519.
19. Rafferty & Shinn, see note 13 above.
20. Kozol, J. (1988). *Rachel and her children: Homeless families in America*. NY: Fawcett Columbine.
21. Kozol, see note 20 above.
22. Goodman, L., Saxe, L., & Harvey, M. (1991). "Homelessness as psychological trauma." *American Psychologist*, 46(11), 1219-1225.
23. Goodman, Saxe, & Harvey, see note 22 above.
24. Goodman, Saxe, & Harvey, see note 22 above.
25. Stern, J. & Urdang, L. (Eds.). (1973). *The Random House Dictionary of the English Language*: NY: Random House.
26. Goodman, Saxe, & Harvey, see note 22.
27. Bassuk & Rubin, see note 3 above; Berne, et al., see note 9 above; Rescorla, L., Parker, R., & Stolley, P. (1991). "Ability, achievement and adjustment in homeless children." American Journal of Orthopsychiatry, 61(2), 210-220.
28. Baumann, S.L. (1993). "The meaning of being homeless." *Scholarly Inquiry for Nursing Practice: An International Journal*, 7(1), 59-73; Heusel, K. (1990). "The experience of homelessness viewed through the eyes of homeless school-age children." (Doctoral dissertation, Ohio State University, 1990). *University Microfilms International*.
29. Faux, S.A., Walsh, M., & Deatrick, J.A. (1988). "Intensive interviewing of children and adolescents." *Western Journal of Nursing Research*, 10(2), 180-193.
30. Deatrick, J. & Faux, S. (1991). "Conducting qualitative studies with children and adolescents." In J.M. Morse (Ed.) *Qualitative Nursing Research*, Newbury Park, CA: Sage.
31. Faux, et al., see note 29 above; Touliatos, J., & Compton, N.H. (1988). *Approaches to Child Study*. Minneapolis, MN: Burgess Publishing.
32. Moustakas, C. (1990). *Heuristic Research*. Newbury Park, CA: Sage Publications.
33. Rossi, P.H., Wright, J., Fisher, G., & Willis, G. (1987). "The urban homeless, estimating composition and size." *Science*, 235, 1336-1341.
34. Stern & Urdang, see note 25 above.
35. Watson, J. (1989). "Human caring and suffering: A subjective model for health sciences." In R. Taylor & J. Watson (Eds.). *They Shall Not Hurt, Human Suffering and Human Caring*. Boulder, CO: Colorado Associated University Press.
36. Watson, see note 35 above.

37. Watson, J. (1988). *Nursing: Human Science and Human Care.* New York: National League for Nursing.

38. Watson, see note 37 above.

39. Watson, see note 37 above.

40. Watson, see note 37 above.

41. Watson, see note 35 above.

42. Watson, see note 37 above.

43. Watson, see note 35 above.

44. Guba, E. (1990). *The Paradigm Dialog.* Newbury Park, CA: Sage Publications.

45. Manicus & Secord cited in Rogers, C. (1989). "A human science." In H. Kirschenbaum & V.L. Henderson (Ed.), *The Carl Rogers Reader.* Boston: Houghton Mifflin Company.

46. Axline, V. (1947). *Play Therapy.* NY, NY: Ballantine Books.

47. Axline, see note 46 above.

48. Delpo, E.G. & Frick, S. (1988). "Directed and nondirected play as therapeutic modalities." *Children's Health Care: Journal of the Association for the Care of Children's Health,* 16, 261-267.

49. Guerney, L.F. (1983). "Client-centered (nondirective) play therapy." In C. Schaefer & K. O'Connor (Eds.). *Handbook of Play Therapy.* NY: John Wiley & Sons.

50. Rogers, C. (1961). *On Becoming a Person.* Boston, MA: Houghton Mifflin Company.

51. Berck, J. (1992). *No place to be: Voices of homeless children.* Boston: Houghton Mifflin Company.

52. Watson, J. (1987). "Academic and clinical collaboration: Advancing the art and science of human caring." *Communicating Nursing Research,* Vol. 20, *Collaboration in Nursing Research: Advancing the Science of Human Care.* Western Institute of Nursing. Proceedings of the Western Society for Research in Nursing Conference, Tempe, AZ, April/May.

II

Review of the Literature

A literature review was conducted to identify research studies which focused on the experience of homeless children, the perspectives of children, and the use of expressive play therapy techniques as a research tool. This chapter is divided into sections concerning these areas. Research findings documenting the health, psychological, and developmental status of homeless children were bracketed by this researcher until the data collection and analysis of the participants' perspectives was completed. [1]

STRUGGLING TO STAY TOGETHER

The majority of homeless families consist of a single mother with two to three minor children.[2] Understanding what is special to homeless children must begin with an attempt at understanding the events that led to the children's arrival at the shelter. The experience of being homeless begins with the loss of a home.

Berne, Dato, Mason and Rafferty maintain that homelessness occurs primarily because of poverty.[3] Bassuk and Rosenberg conducted a study comparing low-income housed mothers with homeless mothers. In both groups, the mothers were on welfare, had little work experience and were currently single and poor. A greater proportion of housed mothers than homeless mothers had been on welfare as children. The housed mothers were generally more adept at obtaining services through the system (i.e. housing and food stamps) than the homeless mothers who had not been on welfare during their childhood. The homeless women had fewer social supports than the housed low-income women, and were more likely to have been abused during childhood. Homeless women were twice as likely to have been involved in an abusing adult relationship, and were more than twice as likely to have been investigated for child abuse themselves. The support networks for housed mothers included significantly more female friends and extended family. The homeless mothers had less contact with their adult support network, and named men more frequently than women as their supports. Twenty-two percent were unable to name any adults in their support network, naming their minor children as their supports instead.[4] Wood conducted a study examining homeless families headed by single women. Of those women involved with men, more than half were involved in relationships with men who were alcoholics, physically abusive, possessed a criminal record, or were mentally ill. Three-fourths of the women reported a history of physical or sexual abuse, with 27% having been removed from their homes as a child.[5] An earlier study by Bassuk, Rubin and Lauriat reported that homeless mothers frequently recounted histories of physical and sexual abuse. Patterns of family disruptions, loss of parents, a lack of work skills, and domestic violence were issues for these mothers. These homeless mothers lacked social supports which may have enabled them to avoid their current situation.[6]

Grigsby, Baumann, Gregorich and Roberts-Gray found that social disaffiliation was a risk factor for homelessness.[7] According to Shinn, Knickman and Weitzman, social isolation is central to homelessness.[8] Reilly found that a common precursor of homelessness was childhood placement in a foster home or serious and chronic childhood abuse.[9] Feelings of powerlessness, low self-esteem, and an inability to trust and form relationships frequently result from a childhood of abuse.[10] Self-esteem and trust are integral to the development of a supportive, loving adult relationship, elements which are clearly missing in an abusive household.[11]

The combination of poverty and a history of victimization are common themes in the lives of homeless adults. In a society with little available housing for poor families, disrupted social ties increase an individuals' vulnerability to homelessness.[12] For many of the poor, there is a fine line between being housed and being homeless. A network of friends and family can provide the help a family needs when an apartment burns down, an illness occurs or a husband leaves. A history of abusive relationships may keep a family from reaching out to others when a crisis occurs. Adults raised in abusive homes may simply not trust that others will helm them when they need help.

It is vitally important to understand the experience of homeless children. At the very least, these children are stigmatized by society for their situation. It is possible that the love, devotion and support of their family will sustain them through nights in overcrowded shelters, and empty, colorless days waiting in line. However, parents who have never experienced the warmth of interpersonal relationships may have trouble convincing their children that it exists. This research study contributes to the growing knowledge base of the experience of homeless people.

Nurses interacting with homeless children will be able to develop a deeper understanding of their experience. Understanding meanings and the human response to experience enhances the nurses' authenticity in the human care process.

"A KID IN A SHELTER"

Few researchers have investigated the experience of homeless children. Authors who have focused on children or who have included children in a larger study of the homeless population have documented significant health and emotional problems.[13]

Wood conducted a descriptive study in an attempt to understand the health needs of homeless families.[14] Delayed immunizations, failure to thrive, delayed growth or obesity, and developmental delays were commonly occurring health problems for the children of these families. Rafferty & Shinn reported a higher incidence of infant mortality among homeless children in New York City than among poor housed children (25 deaths per 1000 live births, compared with 17 per 1000 live births among housed poor women, and 12 per 1000 for women citywide).[15] According to Wright, pediatricians at the New York City Children's Health Project have identified a "homeless child syndrome."[16] The syndrome comprises "poverty related health problems, immunization delays, untreated or undertreated acute and chronic illnesses, unrecognized disorders, school, behavioral, and psychological problems, child abuse and neglect."[17] Parker, Rescorla, Finkelstein, Barnes, Holmes & Stolley conducted a study in Philadelphia with 146 families living in city shelters.[18] Accidents, lead toxicity, anemia, and communicable diseases such as upper respiratory infections and gastroenteritis were the most common health problems reported.[19] Murata, Mace, Strehlow, & Schuler collected data from 303 homeless children's health visits to the UCLA School of Nursing Health Center.[20] Otitis media, communicable diseases, and accidents occurred more frequently in the homeless population than in the housed population when compared with data from the National Ambulatory Medical Care Survey.

In Bassuk & Rubin's study of 156 homeless children in Massachusetts, more than half scored high enough on the Children's Depression Inventory to warrant psychiatric referral.[21] Forty-seven per cent of the 81 children tested with the Denver Developmental Screening Test manifested at least one developmental delay. Both Schulsinger and Davidhizer and Frank found depression, anxiety and learning difficulties were common among homeless school-aged children residing in shelters.[22] Bassuk and Rubin, Parker et al. and Wood found that school failure was a common occurrence in the lives of homeless children.[23]

The experience of homelessness has been viewed as a traumatic event in the life of a child.[24] Children who have experienced a traumatic event often exhibit learning difficulties.[25] "Psychological trauma refers to a set of responses to extraordinary, emotionally overwhelming and personally uncontrollable life events."[26] According to Berne, et al., posttraumatic stress disorder is the most common psychological diagnosis among homeless children.[27]

Whitman, Accardo, Boyert and Kendagor examined the developmental impact of homelessness on 139 children at the Salvation Army Emergency Lodge in St. Louis, Missouri.[28] Serious language and developmental delays were found among the children. According to Whitman,

> these homeless children exhibited a
> developmental pattern more like that
> observed in an abused and neglected
> population than in a normal or a
> mentally retarded population. This
> finding is important because none of
> these children demonstrated any other
> signs of chronic or acute child abuse
> while in the shelter.[29]

Rescorla, Parker, and Stolley conducted a study of 83 homeless children between the ages of 3 and 12 years in Philadelphia shelters.[30] The preschool children exhibited more developmental, language delays and behavior problems than housed preschool children. However, the school-age homeless children were generally similar to housed school-age children. Rescorla, Parker and Stolley suggest that the stable and predictable routine of school had a positive impact on the school-age children's ability to adjust to homelessness. Most of the preschool children were not enrolled in a day care program and spent their days at the shelter.[31]

These research findings reflect a need for research studies which focus on understanding the experience of homeless children. Rescorla, Parker, and Stolley state their study does not imply that homeless school-age children are doing well, children from low-income housed families are not doing well either. Other researchers have documented significant health problems, developmental delays, learning difficulties, anxiety and depression among homeless children.[32] The instability of shelter life, overcrowding, the lack of privacy and routine may contribute to the children's distress along with the detrimental effects of poverty, family violence and parental unemployment. Little is known about the actual experience of being homeless for children. This literature review yielded only one study which attempted to understand the child's experience of homelessness.[33]

A CHILD'S VIEW OF BEING HOMELESS

Heusel conducted a qualitative study with homeless school-aged children living in public shelters.[34] Thirty-three children were asked to describe their experience of homelessness. Heusel found that one-fourth described feeling sad or worried, one-fourth reflected themes of being poor and embarrassed, one-fourth reported that "the experience was alright," and one-fourth were unable to verbalize their feelings. The most common stressful experiences mentioned by the children in Heusel's study were moving frequently, leaving your friends, changing schools, having no place to call home and being ridiculed for being homeless. The most frequently mentioned positive experiences were maintaining a loving relationship with parents, meeting and making new friends, feeling safe and having room to play. Some of the children felt that living in a shelter was preferable to their previous living situation.

The narrow focus of the current literature supports the need for an innovative approach to understanding what is special to homeless children. Previous studies have painted dire pictures of shelter life, but Heusel has revealed that children's perceptions can be very different from the perceptions of researchers.[35] Children's perceptions are an important area for investigation and an area which has been largely neglected in the scientific literature. Fully one-fourth of the children in Heusel's study identified their pre-homeless status as stressful and shelter life as an improvement. This suggests that the depression, developmental delays, anxiety and stress reported in previous studies may not be the consequences of homelessness, but the legacy of growing up poor in America. Heusel acknowledges the problems inherent in interviewing children and recommends the use of play and artwork for data collection with this population.[36]

The present study uncovered what homeless children view as special. The children's own photography was used to explore what was special to them. The purpose of using photography was to provide a structure that children could use to frame their stories. This method encouraged children to unfold their perspectives as they discussed their photographs.

THE MEANINGS OF CHILDREN

A literature search was conducted to identify studies which explored the meanings that children assign to events or situations. No studies were found which addressed this area. Traditionally, children have been studied from the perspective of adults. Teachers or parents have been asked to interpret the meaning of the child's life experience.[37] It has been widely believed that children lacked the developmental maturity and socialization experience to accurately describe and understand their world.[38] However, an alternative view is gaining acceptance. Researchers have found that by using a variety of qualitative techniques, children can provide "valid, meaningful descriptions" of their life experience.[39]

Three articles were identified which focused on the child's perspective of stressful events and psychosocial adaptation. Ryan conducted a study with school-age children to identify their coping strategies.[40] The author stated that "the number and variety of coping strategies and the candor with which they named strategies are evidence that 8 to 12 year old children are capable of reflecting and reporting their own behavior."[41] Issel, Ersek and Lewis studied 6 to 8 year old children living with a mother diagnosed with breast cancer.[42] They recommend that future research studies consider developmental differences and language capabilities of child participants when designing interview questions. Humphreys' study about the worries of children of battered mothers revealed a wide range of concerns.[43] Children expressed fears ranging from those specifically related to battering, to the uncertainty of their mother's condition, abandonment, and health-related concerns. A qualitative descriptive design was used which allowed the expression of a divergent range of concerns.

The paucity of research studies focusing on the perspectives of children reflects a need for research in this area. According to Watson, humans possess unique inner resources and strengths that can be drawn upon to meet health challenges.[44] These inner resources are uncovered as the individual reveals the meaning they assign to their experience. This study is unique in it's focus on the child's experience of what is special. Prior research studies have demonstrated that children are capable of expressing themselves. Qualitative studies enable researchers to access a variety of techniques applicable to the child's developmental and experiential level. For this study, the researcher used methods based on expressive play therapy to communicate more fully with the child-participants.

EXPRESSIVE PLAY THERAPY

The term "play therapy" refers to the purposeful use of play to facilitate communication.[45] The term expressive play therapy is used to describe play therapy methods which incorporate art and creative materials.[46] Play is the child's natural medium of expression. During play, a child explores, constructs, understands and assimilates the world. The content, theme and process of spontaneous play provide information about the child's thoughts, beliefs and feelings.[47] An important aspect of play is the chance to experiment with a broad range of behavior. According to Kramer, this is particularly valuable to species which must adapt to changing environments.[48] Play provides a chance to "try on" behaviors and activities before they are necessary. Play involves the use of a toy or object whose function is predetermined.[49] There is no goal to play, but an "unending back and forth." Children play randomly and will often play the same scene over and over from different perspectives.[50]

Play therapists often use art materials in addition to toys in their play room. An art activity can encourage self-expression and the representation of feelings and ideas.[51] Frequently, children are reluctant to talk about their experience or they do not possess a vocabulary that enables them to describe their ideas. These children may find it easier to express themselves through an artistic medium, which may be a less problematic and more spontaneous means of communication.[52] Children's drawings are a useful communication tool.[53] Drawing can reduce the child's anxiety level by involving the child in a familiar task.[54]

Psychoanalytically oriented therapists, such as Anna Freud or Margaret Naumburg, advocate the use of projective interpretation of children's drawings to understand the relationship between the content of the drawings and the child's unconscious feelings and thoughts.[55] This type of interpretation is flawed by its inability to reveal the child's unique understanding and representation of the subject matter. A humanistic, child-centered approach will encourage the child to interpret the drawings.[56] The artwork is viewed as a personal metaphor for the individual's perception of reality.[57]

It is precisely this creation of symbolic meaning that makes expressive play therapy such a rich avenue for qualitative research. Wadeson discussed the difficulty of attempting qualitative research in this area.[58] The greatest difficulty Dr. Wadeson encountered was attempting objective measurement of the artwork

> . . . objective measurement of the latter is possible only if simple, formal elements of the work are separated out. Since the whole art work is more than the sum of its parts, such a breakdown may turn out to defeat its purpose . . . our understanding of content may be enriched by the creator's explanation

of an art work's meaning, but
explanations are hard to codify.[59]

It is true that the subjective expression of an art experience would be difficult to study using quantitative methods. Qualitative methods are useful when the research question requires the uncovering of meanings. In qualitative research, objectivity is neither sought nor desired. An attempt is made to understand the phenomenon in it's entirety.[60] The goal of qualitative research is to understand, explain and to discover meanings within experiences. The meaning of experience for the individual is of paramount importance.[61] In the understanding of the experience, the whole is more than the sum of the parts.[62] It is not possible to understand the meaning of an experience by splitting it into parts and measuring the results.

Photography

Photography has many of the same elements of drawing, except that it is a medium in which every child can feel immediate success. This researcher's preliminary work with children and cameras demonstrated the ease and familiarity that children display with cameras even if they had never used one before (preliminary work is discussed in chapter 3). Furnishing children with a camera provides an insider's view of their world.[63] The photographer structures the image taken by the camera, so that what is seen is a reflection of the photographer's interpretations. "It must be emphasized that pictures are not unambiguous records of reality. The sense viewers make of them depends upon cultural assumptions, personal knowledge and the context in which the picture is presented."[64] There are three aspects of photographic analysis according to Ball and Smith: 1) the content of the photograph 2) the referent, or what it is a picture of and 3) the context in which it is described.[65] When these aspects are considered together, the full value of the picture is appreciated.

Touliatos and Compton compared verbal interviews with interviews using photographs.[66] They found the respondents exhibited greater interest and gave more information during the photographic interviews. Collier and Collier found that photographs invite free expression.[67] The photograph becomes a third party to the interview. This enables the investigator and participant to truly become co-participants as they explore the photograph. The photograph and not the participant is the object of the study. Finally, the participants are able to spontaneously tell their own stories.

Wolf found the use of photographs initiated discussions which "ultimately elicit significant material."[68] Nonverbal communication often contains unconscious material which the person can use to develop a greater self-awareness. Wolf's study used photography with "underachieving adolescents," their chronic fear of failure contributed to a resistance to even the most simple drawing exercises. With photography, the image is readily produced. The photography held the attention of the adolescents, and allowed them to focus on themselves in a non-threatening way.[69] Through the reproductive, communicative, and creative nature of photography, individuals can develop a greater understanding of themselves.[70] The search for the meaning of experience is enhanced by methods which allow individuals to achieve a greater understanding of themselves.

In this research study, children used photography to explore and describe what was special to them. Photography was used to encourage the children to fully express their ideas, and to provide a focus for the interview questions.

PRELIMINARY WORK

Once the photographic method and the concept of special evolved, a preliminary study was conducted to test the method. Six children were asked to take pictures of what was special to them. In this project, 3 boys and 3 girls between the ages of 9 and 11 years from middle class, two parent families were selected to participate. These children met as a group for two, one hour interviews.

Parents were contacted by telephone. Once both parent and child gave verbal consent, the researcher made an appointment to discuss the study in detail with them. At this meeting, consents were signed, the study was explained in detail, and the child-participants were given the camera. Disposable Polaroid 35 Cameras with Flash were used. The children were instructed in the use of the camera and they were asked to take pictures of anything they thought of as meaningful or "special" to them. The children were given 72 hours to complete the assignment of taking all 24 pictures. At the end of the 72 hour period, the cameras were collected and the film developed. Two days later, the six children met together to view and discuss their photographs as a group. A structured interview guide was followed by the researcher as described in Appendix F. The children were asked to select the five photographs which they found the most special and these were marked by the researcher. The five special photographs were enlarged to 5x7 photos. The next group interview was held two days after the first one, to allow time to process the photographs. During this group interview, the children were animated and excited. Their initial reluctance to talk about their work appeared to have vanished. They were asked to view their enlarged photos and rank them from the most special to least special. Then the researcher asked them to discuss the "top 5" pictures in greater detail.

The discussions were audiotaped and field notes were taken. A log of methodological decisions, and a reflexive journal were kept by the researcher. When all of the data was gathered, the audiotapes were transcribed. Audiotapes, field notes and the photographs were unitized, sorted and analyzed for themes. The children are not identified by their real names to protect their confidentiality.

Results From Preliminary Work

A total of 131 (91%) out of 144 photographs were returned from the developer. Of the 24 pictures taken by each child-participant, an average of 22 were successfully processed. One child-participant received all 24 of her pictures and one received only 17 (he forgot to use the flash indoors). The child-participants were asked to group their pictures into four categories. The children chose their own categories which are indicated in Table 1.

Table 1 Categories of Photographs by Content		
Categories	# of photographs	% of total
things I made or won	11	8.4%
important places I go	32	24.4%
special things	42	32.1%
special people and animals	46	35.1%
Total	131	100.0%

The child-participants were asked to select the five pictures that were the most special to them of all of their photographs. These pictures were enlarged. (See Table II). Two of the children selected group photographs of their families as the most special picture, two of the children selected a picture of their mother as their most special picture (interestingly, these were the two children with step-fathers), and two children selected a picture of themselves as their most special picture.

Table II Top Five Most Special Photographs Selected		
Categories	# of photographs	% of total
things I made or won	2	6.6%
important places I go	3	10.0%
special things	4	13.3%
special people and animals	21	70.1%
Total	30	100.0%

Discussion of Preliminary Work

Several themes emerged from the data. The first one was "feeling understood." Two of the children identified their grand-parents as "someone who helps me or listens to my problems." Sue identified a family friend who is her "adopted" grandmother because "she always helps me." Donna didn't have a chance to take a picture of her aunt, but talked about her as a "special person" who listens to me. Pictures of grandparents and special friends were placed in the top 5 usually right behind pictures of parents.

The next theme was "belonging." Being a part of a family, belonging to a church, having friends were all important pictures for the child-participants. Two children took their cameras to school and four children took pictures of their friends. The importance of belonging was emphasized by Donna:

> if I didn't have friends I certainly,
> probably wouldn't like myself very
> much because if people don't like me I
> must be pretty stupid.

For some of the children, "survival" was an important theme. An overriding concern for survival seemed to permeate Scott's pictures and descriptions. He had taken two pictures of his toys and collections and one picture of his drawings. The remainder of his pictures included one of his family, his grandmother and objects necessary for shelter, food and clothing. Scott's most important picture was of his parents who were special because "they provide me with clothing and food." Scott also included, in his top five pictures, a photograph of his closet and his clothes. Not included in the top five but still striking was his description of his house:

> well, another thing that is important
> to me is my house. It gives me shelter
> and whenever if I was sleeping out
> with the stars probably I would get
> cold for one thing, and animals and
> ants would be crawling all over me.

Scott had the widest variety of objects in his pictures. They included the kitchen, the family telephone, the TV, the washing machine, bathroom, air conditioner, cars, light bulbs:

> and a picture of some trees because
> they provide oxygen for us.

Some of Donna's descriptions of her photographs revealed anxiety about survival, a lack of certainty that she would be care for:

> My second one, which is my family,
> because they are my family and I don't
> know what I would do without them.
> I'd probably be lying on the street
> dead. My parents pay for everything
> for me, not everything but most
> everything. I don't pay for my food. I
> don't pay for my clothes. Well
> sometimes I do.
>
> This is a picture of my kitchen,
> because it gives me food.

With survival came the category of "certainty vs uncertainty." The children whose pictures revealed a concern about survival seemed to lack a certainty that the adults in their lives would take care of them. Children who did not mention clothes, food or shelter as important topics took pictures of their toys. This suggests a certainty that their survival needs would be met and their attention could be placed on developing autonomy and self-knowledge. The focus of Scott's pictures suggests an uncertainty that the adults in his life will take care of him. This lack of certainty may be described as being apart or separate. Separateness, if excessive, may lead to feelings of uncertainty. Mayeroff speaks of basic certainty as "being rooted in the world . . . a deep-seated security . . . having a good sense of our own worth."[71]

The last theme derived from the data was one that encompasses the other themes, that of connecting vs separating. I was initially surprised that none of the children said "my parents are special because they love me." There was only one child who said "my family is always there for me, no matter what." An essential task of family life is the establishment of a pattern of separation and connectedness.[72] Family interactions may be expressed as connecting-separating. This concept describes the balance between family members and their roles, within and outside of the family. This coming together and pulling apart seems to happen almost simultaneously. The rhythms are synchronized for each family unit. According to Parse, "connecting-separating is the rhythmical process of distancing and relating, that is, moving in one direction and away from others yet always toward greater diversity."[73] Families grow and change through their relationships with the outside environment, yet continue to maintain their unique identity.

Nadine had strong family supports in the form of grandparents who "help me a lot" and family friends who "are always there to help us." Nadine's other pictures were of her pet hamster, toys, sports equipment, and awards she'd won. Items that were hers alone, which helped to establish her autonomy from her family.

Jason took a picture of his bicycle and placed it in his top five pictures. Jason used his bicycle to get away from his house. He emphasized friends more than any other participant, although they were not included among his most meaningful pictures. Developmentally, an 11 year old should be separating from his family and placing a greater emphasis on friends. The key psychosocial growth issues in this age group are separation and independence, cognitive expansion, sexual identity, moral maturation and preparation for an adult role in society.[74] His top five pictures demonstrated connectedness and separateness. They included his mom, his stepdad, his dog, his collections and trophies and his bicycle.

Donna had a special place that she cherished in her backyard. It was a place for her to be alone, separate from her family or friends when she needed to.

Sue seemed to feel strong connections to others. Her top five pictures were pictures of "myself, my mother, my adopted grandmother, the playhouse my daddy built for me, and the pool that my parent's gave me." All five of Sue's pictures were focused on either people who cared for her or special things that had been created for her. Sue also took a picture of a favorite tree that reminded her of a friend's sick mother.

Connecting-separating is an important issue for divorced and blended families. Jason said very little about his stepfather, choosing to talk about his father instead. Jason did not take a picture father although he saw him over the picture taking weekend:

> uh, well, my Dad is my most special thing but I didn't get a picture of him, I would have put him in if I had the room and my mom she's the first. She would probably be in there with my Dad.

In David's top five photographs, there was a picture of his mother, his stepdad, his baby sister and the two family dogs. David's other pictures included friends, awards, toys, sports equipment, and a picture of an old photograph of his grandparents. These pictures seem to show a balance between connection to family and age-appropriate independence. David's descriptions of his photographs did not reveal any concern or lack of certainty that his survival needs would be met.

The themes of connectedness-separateness appeared clearly in the data. Related themes of belonging, feeling understood, survival and certainty vs uncertainty were also discerned. Continuing engagement with this data and enlarging the study would contribute to a more complete understanding of the meaning and appropriateness of these themes. The children's photographic self-portraits reveal that what is meaningful to them is: connecting and separating with certainty and uncertainty from significant others.

The completion of the preliminary study provided the researcher with a clearer understanding of the concept of special and the use of photography as a research technique. The preliminary work successfully demonstrated that children could use photography to describe what is special to them.

Summary

Research studies involving children as informants are rare in the literature. Studies which investigate children's perceptions are even less common, and studies which investigate what is special to children are non-existent. This may be partly attributable to a commonly held belief that children are unable to describe their world, and in part because there are few successful research methods available for children. Effective research studies require the full participation of the participants. Photography, as was used in this study, is one method of involving children more completely in the research process. The result of this involvement was thicker, richer data.

NOTES

1. Patton, M.Q. (1980). *Qualitative Evaluation and Research Methods*. Newbury Park, CA: Sage Publications.

2. Bassuk, E. & Rubin, L. (1987). "Homeless children: A neglected population." *American Journal of Orthopsychiatry*, 57 (2), 279-286; Rossi, P.H. (1989). "Down and Out in America". Chicago: University of Chicago Press; Schulsinger, E. (1990). "Needs of sheltered homeless children." *Journal of Pediatric Health Care*, 4(3), 136-140; Wright, J.D. (1991). "Children in and of the streets: Health, social policy and the homeless young." *American Journal of Diseases of Children*, 145, 516-519.

3. Berne, A.S., Dato, C., Mason, D.J., & Rafferty, M. (1990). "A nursing model for addressing the health needs of homeless families." *Image*, 22 (1), 8-13.

4. Bassuk, E.L., & Rosenberg, L. (1988). "Why does family homelessness occur? A case-control study." *American Journal of Public Health*, 78 (7), 783-788.

5. Wood, D. (1989). "Homeless children: Their evaluation and treatment." *Journal of Pediatric Health Care*, 3(4), 194-199.

6. Bassuk, E.L., Rubin, L., & Lauriat, M.A. (1986). "Characteristics of sheltered homeless families." *American Journal of Public Health*, 76 (9), 1097-1101.

7. Grigsby, C., Baumann, D., Gregorich, S.E. & Roberts-Gray, C. (1990). "Disaffiliation to entrenchment: A model for understanding homelessness." *Journal of Social Issues*, 46(4), 141-156.

8. Shinn, M., Knickman, J.R., & Weitzman, B.C. (1991). "Social relationships and vulnerability to becoming homeless among poor families." *American Psychologist*, 46(11), 1180-1187.

9. Grigsby, et. al., see note 7 above.

10. Ammerman, R.T., Cassissi, J.E., Hersen, M. & Van Hasselt, V.B. (1986). "Consequences of physical abuse and neglect in children." *Clinical Psychology Review*, 6, 291-310; Beitchman, J.H., Zucker, K.J, Hood, J.E., DaCosta, G.A., Akman, D. & Cassavia, E. (1992). "A review of the long term effects of child sexual abuse." *Child Abuse and Neglect*, 16, 101-118; Blount, K. (1992). "Chronic psychological manifestations." In S. Ludwig & A. Kornberg (Eds.), *Child Abuse: A Medical Reference*. NY, NY: Churchill Livingstone; Green, A.H. (1985). "Children traumatized by physical abuse." In S. Eth & R.S. Pynoos (Eds.), *Post-traumatic Stress Disorder in Children*. Washington, DC: American Psychiatric Press, Inc.; Tower, C.C. (1989). *Understanding Child Abuse and Neglect*. Boston: Allyn and Bacon.

11. Satir, V. (1983). *Conjoint Family Therapy.* Palo Alto, CA: Science and Behavior Books.

12. Shinn, M., et al., see note 8 above.

13. Molnar, J., Rath, W., & Klein, T. (1990). "Constantly compromised: The impact of homelessness of children." *Journal of Social Issues,* 46 (4), 109-123.

14. Wood, see note 5 above.

15. Rafferty, Y. & Shinn, M. (1991). "The impact of homelessness of children." *American Psychologist,* 46 (11), 1170-1179.

16. Wright, see note 2 above.

17. Wright, see note 2 above.

18. Parker, R.M., Rescoria, L.A., Finkelstein, J.A., Barnes, N., Holmes, J.H. & Stolley, P.D. (1991). "A survey of the health of homeless children in Philadelphia shelters." *American Journal of Diseases of Children,* 145, 520-526.

19. Parker, et al., see note 18 above.

20. Murata, J., Mace, J.P., Strehlow, A., & Shuler, P. (1992). "Disease patterns in homeless children: A comparison with national data." *Journal of Pediatric Nursing,* 7(3), 196-202.

21. Bassuk & Rubin, see note 2 above.

22. Schulsinger, see note 2 above; Davidhizar, R. & Frank, B. (1992). "Understanding the physical and psychosocial stressors of the child who is homeless." *Pediatric Nursing,* 18(6), 559-562.

23. Bassuk & Rubin, see note 2 above; Parker, et al. see note 18 above; Wood, see note 5 above.

24. Goodman, L., Saxe, L., & Harvey, M. (1991). "Homelessness as psychological trauma." *American Psychologist,* 46(11), 1219-1225; Shinn, see note 8 above.

25. Eth, S. & Pynoos, R.S. (1985). *Post-traumatic Stress Disorder in Children.* Washington, D.C.: American Psychiatric Press, Inc.

26. Goodman, see note 24 above.

27. Berne, see note 3 above.

28. Whitman, B.Y., Accardo, P., Boyert, M. & Kendagor, R. (1990). "Homelessness and cognitive performance in children: A possible link." *Social Work,* 35(6), 516-519.

29. Whitman, see note 28 above.

30. Rescorla, L., Parker, R., & Stolley, P. (1991). "Ability, achievement, and adjustment in homeless children." *American Journal of Orthopsychiatry,* 61(2), 210-220.

31. Rescorla, see note 30 above.

32. Wood, see note 5 above; Rassuk and Rubin, see note 2 above: Davidhizar and Frank, see note 22 above.

33. Heusel, R.J. (1990). "The experience of homelessness viewed through the eyes of homeless school-age children." (Doctoral dissertation, Ohio State University, 1990). *University Microfilms International*.

34. Heusel, see note 33 above.

35. Heusel, see note 34 above.

36. Heusel, see note 34 above.

37. Deatrick, J. & Faux, S. (1991). "Conducting qualitative studies with children and adolescents." In J.M. Morse (Ed.) *Qualitative Nursing Research*. Newbury Park, CA: Sage; Touliatos, J. & Compton, N.H. (1988). *Approaches to Child Study*. Minneapolis, MN: Burgess Publishing Company.

38. Deatrick & Faux, see note 37 above; Touliatos & Compton, see note 37 above.

39. Deatrick & Faux, see note 37 above.

40. Ryan, N. (1989). "Stress-coping strategies identified from school age children's perspective. *Research in Nursing and Health*, 11-122.

41. Ryan, see note 40 above.

42. Issel, L., Ersek, M. & Lewis, F. (1990). "How children cope with mother's breast cancer." *Oncology Nursing Forum*, 17(3), 5-13.

43. Humphreys, J. (1991). "Children of battered women: Worries about their mothers." *Pediatric Nursing*, 17(4), 342-346.

44. Watson, J. (1988). *Nursing: Human Science and Human Care*. New York, NY: National League for Nursing.

45. Delpo, E.G. & Erick, S. (1988). "Directed and nondirected play as therapeutic modalities." *Children's Health Care: Journal of the Association for the Care of Children's Health*, 16, 261-267.

46. Gladdings, S. (1993). "Poetry and creative writing." In P. Paisley (Ed.), *Expressive Arts and Play Media in Counseling*. Symposium conducted at Appalachian State University, Boone, NC.

47. Delpo & Frick, see note 45 above.

48. Kramer, E. (1977). "Art therapy and play." *American Journal of Art Therapy*, 17, 3-11.

49. Roth, E.A., & Barrett, R.P. (1980). "Parallels in art and play therapy with a disturbed retarded child." *The Arts in Psychotherapy*, 7, 19-26.

50. Kramer, see note 48 above.

51. Nickerson, E. (1983). "Art as a play therapeutic medium." In C.E. Schaefer & K.J. O'Connor (Eds.), *Handbook of Play Therapy*. New York: John Wiley & Sons; Thomas, G.V. & Silk, A. (1990). *An Introduction to the Psychology of Children's Drawings*. NY, NY: University Press.

52. Thomas & Silk, see note 51 above; Case, C. & Dalley, T. (1992). *The Handbook of Art Therapy.* New York: Routledge.

53. Case & Dailey, see note 52 above; Deatrick & Faux, see note 37 above; Denehy, J.A. (1990). "Communicating with children through drawings." In M.J. Craft & J.A. Denehy (Eds.) *Nursing Interventions for Infants and Children.* Phila., PA: W.B. Saunders Co.; Faux, S.A., Walsh, M., Deatrick, J.A. (1988). "Intensive interviewing of children and adolescents." *Western Journal of Nursing Research,* 10(2), 180-193; Nickerson, see note 51 above; Thomas & Silk, see note 51 above.

54. Faux, et al., see note 53 above.

55. Nickerson, see note 51 above.

56. Nickerson, see note 51 above.

57. Johnson,

58. Wadeson, H. (1978). "Art therapy data in research." *American Journal of Art Therapy,* 18, 11-18.

59. Wadeson, see note 58 above.

60. Patton, M.Q. (1980). *Qualitative Evaluation and Research Methods.* Newbury Park, CA: Sage Publications.

61. Guba, E. (1990). *The Paradigm Dialog.* Newbury Park, CA: Sage Publications, Inc.

62. Haase, J.E. & Myers, S.T. (1988). "Reconciling paradigm assumptions of qualitative and quantitative research." *Western Journal of Nursing Research,* 10(2), 128-137.

63. Denzin, N.K. (1989). *The Research Act.* Englewood Cliffs, NJ: Prentice Hall.

64. Ball, M.S. & Smith, G.W. (1992). *Analyzing Visual Data.* Newbury Park, CA: Sage Publications.

65. Ball & smith, see note 64 above.

66. Touliatos, J. & Compton, N.H. (1988). *Approaches to Child Study.* Minneapolis, MN: Burgess Publishing Co.

67. Collier, J. & Collier, M. (1986). *Visual Anthropology: Photography as a Research Method.* Albuquerque, NM: University of New Mexico Press.

68. Wolf, R. (1976). "The Polaroid technique: Spontaneous dialogues from the unconscious." *Art Psychotherapy,* 3, 197-214.

69. Wolf, see note 68 above.

70. Hogan, P.T. (1981). "Phototherapy in the educational setting." *The Arts in Psychotherapy,* 8, 193-199; Zwick, D. (1978). "Photography as a tool toward increased awareness of the aging self." *Art Psychotherapy,* 5, 135-141.

71. Mayeroff, M. (1972). *On Caring.* NY, NY: Harper Collins Publishing.

72. Gillis, C., Highley, B., Roberts, B., & Martinson, I. (1989). *Toward a Science of Family Nursing.* Menlo Park, CA: Addison Wesley Publishing Company.
73. Parse, R.R. (1987). *Nursing Science.* Phila., PA: W.B. Saunders Co.
74. Dixon, S., & Stern, M. (1992). *Encounters with Children: Pediatric Behavior and Development.* Boston: Mosby Year Book.

III

Method

The purpose of this study was to portray and describe what homeless children regard as special through the use of Moustakas' heuristic qualitative method. This chapter describes the design, sampling procedures, interview process, and data analysis used in this study.

In Jean Watson's conceptualization of Human Care, the nurse co-participates with the person in caring. The commitment to care is embedded in understanding meanings and the subjective human response to experience. [1] From this framework, study participants are co-participants with the investigator as they explore and explain their unique perspective. In this study, the term child-participant is used to emphasize the central position of children as co-participants in the investigation.

There are specific challenges inherent in conducting interviews with children. Faux, Walsh, and Deatrick identified three major issues of concern when using children as research subjects. [2] Traditional adult-child communication patterns encourage children to "read" the investigator and give the correct response. This becomes an issue when investigators are attempting to generate credible data. Encouraging children to "tell their own stories" instead of dominating them with a list of questions, will have a profound effect on the research generated. Children, even of the same age, have different cognitive and verbal skills. They may not understand the questions as stated, but in an attempt to please the adult investigator they will select an answer from those provided, significantly reducing the credibility of the study. Encouraging children to "tell their own stories" using a medium that is comfortable for them enables children to express their perspective. Another concern when interviewing children is that they may become tired or bored with the interview. [3] The investigator must be alert for nonverbal cues that indicate fatigue and complete the interview as quickly as possible.[4]

In order to understand and explore children's perspectives, a qualitative method congruent with Watson's conceptualization of Human Care was chosen. Human health goals can be met through "finding meaning in one's existence, discovering inner power and control, and potentiating instances of transcendence and self-healing."[5] Moustakas' heuristic qualitative research design was chosen because this approach stresses dialogue between co-participants, "where each seeks to be experienced and confirmed by the other."[6] The meanings of human experience are sought. Individuality and uniqueness are valued with a focus on the internal processing of the person as the primary way of understanding human experience.

Another important component of heuristic design is the self-knowledge and experience of the investigator. This is related to Watson's carative factor "sensitivity to self and others."[7] Only through a more complete understanding of one's self can nurses become more authentic and sensitive in their interactions with others.[8] The heuristic method requires the investigator's personal involvement in the exploration of the phenomenon. This is termed a self-dialogue, "allowing the phenomenon to speak directly to one's own experience."[9] It is the critical beginning, the initial step of the heuristic process. Childhood is a universal experience, so it is natural to study childhood from a heuristic perspective.

A heuristic method is particularly appropriate for understanding the meanings of children within Watson's framework. Watson emphasizes respect for the knowledge and understanding of the individual. Too frequently, children are overwhelmed and intimidated by the adults around them. They must remember to mind their manners, listen carefully to teachers, do homework, obey parents, with frequently little time left for their own ideas or self-expression. Within a heuristic method, children are able to "teach" the researcher. The children's thoughts and opinions are directly sought and valued. Heuristic methods also grant a wide range of creative expression. Children may be reluctant to talk about their experiences, or they may not possess a vocabulary which enables them to clearly express their ideas. These children may find it easier to express themselves through an artistic medium used as data in a heuristic study.

HEURISTIC INQUIRY

Heuristic research methods were derived by Moustakas through reflection, intuition and self-discovery.[10] These ideas were focused and developed during Moustaka's initial heuristic project on the study of loneliness.[11] The goal of heuristic research is to discover the nature of a human problem or phenomenon and to explicate it as it exists while retaining the essence of the person in the experience.[12] This method requires the full participation of the investigator. Derived from the Greek word heuretikos, the word heuristic means "I find." According to Moustakas, "it refers to a process of internal search through which one discovers the nature and meaning of experience and develops methods and procedures for further investigation and analysis."[13] This search begins with the self and through a passionate, disciplined commitment evolves beyond the subjective into a systematic and definitive exposition of the question.[14]

There is no prescribed design as each search is unique in it's attempt to bring a humanistic understanding to human existence and behavior. This focus on recreating the experience of the individual may lead the investigator to unconventional sources of data, such as the use of photographs. Understanding the experience of children, through the eyes of children, requires the development of non-traditional methods. Traditional methods are problematic for children who may have learned to be wary of adult questions and intimidated by adult authority. Photography is a method that allows children to express themselves freely and thus become the expert as they interpret their own words. This approach simultaneously empowers and enhances the child's self-knowledge, while providing a glimpse of childhood experience.

Monstakas describes six phases of heuristic research: a) initial engagement; b) immersion; c) incubation; d) illumination e) explication; f) culmination.[15] These phases are described in relation to this study.

Initial Engagement

In a heuristic study, the initial engagement phase precedes the development of the question. Personal involvement in the research question may begin long before a question is even considered. The task of initial engagement is "to discover an intense interest, a passionate concern that calls out to the researcher."[16] Through self-dialogue, intuition, and a commitment to enter fully into the theme the question achieves form and significance. The heuristic process emphasizes indwelling, intuition, and the investigator's internal frame of reference.[17]

The investigator's personal experience with the phenomenon is essential in a heuristic study. However, a similar experience will allow the investigator to use the content of his/her experience to understand the context of the research question.[18] I was not homeless as a child. However, my father was frequently out of work, and we moved every few years from one part of the country to another. I learned to form quick, temporary relationships and to always be prepared for change. Nothing was ever certain, and I never believed that anything would last for more than a few months.

For this study, I used the content of my experience (of having been a child in a family always searching for a new home) to understand the context of the experience of others (of being a child in a family without a home). In this way, using content to understand the particular context of the research situation, the investigator can use inner resources and personal knowledge of internal processes to understand what is meaningful in the experience of another.

The Beginning

For me this process began 20 years ago when I was a nursing student learning to give immunizations to children at an inner-city clinic in New Orleans, La. In an institutional gray building surrounded by housing projects, the patients and their parents waited to be seen by the clinic staff. The children were barefoot, their clothes dirty and often torn or too small. There were no toys available so the children played and fought with each other. Their mothers sat passively staring at the floor. It seemed that there must be something more that we could do than immunize these children. I wondered what growing up in the projects was like, how did the children experience their world, how was their childhood going to affect their lives? As I continued to work with underserved populations as a nurse and a nurse practitioner, I was frequently impressed and delighted by the core of resiliency, love, and devotion that I witnessed in many families. Again, I wondered how the children understood their experience, what was important and meaningful to them? As I became a mother, I was able to witness firsthand the growth and development of children. Their rapidly changing perspective is fascinating.

In my own life, though never homeless, there was a time of great uncertainty. My husband and I married the day after he graduated from college. A week later, we packed everything we owned into our car and drove across the country. Arriving in Philadelphia during the coldest winter since colonial times, we had only light jackets and little money. We stayed briefly with my aunt, but spent the days combing the city for jobs and an apartment. It wasn't long before we realized that we could not rent an apartment without a job, and we could not get a job without an address. Fortunately, being young, optimistic and energetic we were able to convince a real estate agent to rent us an apartment based on our potential earnings. It was frightening to realize that even as a nurse there were few to no jobs in Philadelphia that winter. Without jobs we were lost. We had no friends. only very distant family, and very limited money. Suddenly, I understood how very easy it would be to become homeless.

These experiences, along with my own childhood experiences, led me to an interest in studying the lives of homeless children. In preparation for this study I read books and articles about homelessness, participated in a University of South Carolina, College of Nursing research study on the health needs of the homeless in South Carolina[19] and watched children's films and videos related to searching for a home.

Immersion

During this phase, the investigator becomes totally involved with the research question. "The researcher lives the questions in waking, sleeping, and even dream states. Everything in his or her life becomes crystallized around the question . . . "[20]

The immersion phase for this study began with a play therapy course which introduced the researcher to play therapy theory and techniques. In play therapy the child's natural medium of expression becomes a therapeutic tool. This investigator was seeking techniques which could be adapted to research to uncover the experience of children. The investigator's practicum for the play therapy course was in a shelter for homeless families. In the course of the play therapy practicum the investigator began using photography to add a different dimension to play therapy sessions. This investigator was impressed and delighted at the ease the children displayed while taking and describing their photographs during play sessions. Other children responded enthusiastically when asked if they wanted to take pictures.

Special

Once this investigator became convinced that photography was a valid method for accessing the perspectives of children it became necessary to develop a concept which children could readily understand. The concept of meaningful is not a term that children readily understand. The term "special" was uncovered during a discussion with the researcher's 9 year old daughter. While attempting to translate the phenomenon under consideration for this study to a term understood by children, Laura came into the study and I asked her "if something is really important to you what would you call it?" She replied, "That's easy, I'd call it special." I learned a very important but frequently forgotten lesson that day, when studying children it is vitally important to talk to children.

The term special is often an unfamiliar concept to adults. Adults tend to use the term to describe what is on sale at the market. However, it is a concept frequently used and understood by children. Subsequent preliminary discussions with children confirmed Laura's viewpoint. Other children immediately understood the meaning of "special." When asked to respond to the question, "what is something special?", children frequently expressed the idea that special is "something that is really close to you, that you love deeply or care about", "something you care about a lot," "something that means a lot to someone," "something meaningful" and "something that you're going to keep for a real long time." These definitions are similar to the adult concept of meaningful.

When children describe what is special they reveal what has meaning for them. According to Parse, "structuring meaning multidimensionally is cocreating reality through the languaging of valuing and imaging."[21] The words the children choose uncover their values. The meanings they have assigned to their reality are revealed in the course of their discussions.

Incubation

Time for frequent rest periods are essential to the research design. Often insights occur when the investigator is not fully involved with the material, but has achieved some distance from the data. The amount of time needed for incubation is variable and depends on study characteristics.[22]

Illumination

When the investigator is open and receptive to tacit knowledge and intuition, illumination will occur as a new awareness.[23] Snyder describes this phase as "the period of new light."[24] There is a breakthrough, which is not only thought but felt. Deeper meanings and insights are revealed. The components of the question separate into themes and essences. Nuances which were once hidden become visible.

Explication

This is the period of pulling together all of the understandings, feelings, intuitions, and thoughts into a composite depiction. The investigator includes data collected from co-participants, logs, and bibliographic references.[25] It is a time of indwelling and focusing in order to fully understand the meaning of the experience. The investigator must be aware that explication comes from within. The investigator's internal frame of reference is utilized to discover the meaning of the phenomenon. The composite depiction of the core experience is then made explicit through detailed description.[26]

Culmination

The culmination is a creative synthesis of the meanings and details of the experience with the intuition and tacit understanding of the investigator. Snyder describes this phase as " . . . a shift occurs. Having developed an understanding in a deeply felt sense that goes beyond words, the investigator is now able to see and feel a truth where none existed before . . . It is a creative statement of a whole new reality."[27] This portrayal may be represented as metaphor, poetry, art, music, stories or the written word.

RESEARCH PROCEDURE

The research procedure entailed 10 systematic steps. These included: a) obtaining permission to conduct the study at the shelter and consents from parents and child-participants; b) collecting demographic data; c) conducting the first interview session; d) processing of photographs; e) investigator review of the photographs; f) second interview session with selection by children of their five special pictures; g) enlarging the special pictures; h) third interview session and debriefing session; i) obtaining consent from shelter residents to use photographs in publication or presentations; j) presentation of photographs to residents and shelter director.

Sample

The sample consisted of 12 children between the ages of 6 and 12 years who were residing in a shelter for homeless families in a city in South Carolina. Children participating in the study met the following criteria: a) spoke and understood English; b) were willing to participate in the study; c) had a parent or guardian who was willing for the child to participate in the study.

A total of 18 interviews were conducted. Initially there were 4 groups of children with 3 members each. However, as the study progressed the groups changed and three children were interviewed singly. Two child-participants had difficulty with the camera and only 12 pictures were returned from the developer. They were given a second camera, and the operation of the camera was reviewed. Only the photographs from the second attempt were used in subsequent interviews with these children.

Setting

The study was conducted in a private, non-profit shelter for homeless families located in a central South Carolina city. The shelter houses between 14 and 16 families at a time. Each family occupies one room. There are communal bathrooms. Occasionally, families are "doubled up" in a room, if the families are very small (i.e. one mother and one small child). Meals are served in a commons room, which also serves as a meeting room, a homework room, and a recreation hall. A full-time social worker was available to assist families with the location of permanent housing and jobs. There was a small day-care for young children that was staffed by volunteers. There was an after-school and summer program for school-age children.

Families could stay at the shelter for a period of 90 days. Parents expected to actively pursue permanent housing, jobs, or education during their stay. The shelter staff provided support, information and counseling. Attendance at weekly resident meetings was mandatory for the adults. These meetings provided a time to discuss group living issues, questions, or community resources. Frequently, a representative of an outside agency was available to discuss programs with the residents. Curfew for adults and children was six o'clock in the evening. Guests were allowed one visitor during the day, but at curfew all guests left the premises. Parents were expected to supervise their children at all times, unless prior arrangements had been made. The staff arranged transportation to the local public school, and provided day care for younger children, and an after-school program. At the time of the study, there were 12 children, between the ages of 6 and 12 years, in residence at the shelter.

Interview Sessions

This study was conducted over an eight day period at the shelter. Each child participated in three group or single interview sessions. The child-participants in this study were initially assigned to small groups of three for the interview sessions. Each child met with the investigator three times, although not necessarily with the same group. For purposes of group management, there were no more than three children in each group.[28] The children were placed into groups based on their age. Developmentally, physically, and intellectually there are often great differences between children more than one to two years apart in age. When children are close to each other in age, they function more effectively as a group.[29] Group members were only one to two years apart in age. The purpose of group interview sessions was to encourage the children to feel comfortable with the investigator. Children may be inhibited by one-to-one contact with adults. A group of peers provides feelings of safety and security for children, especially if they are uncomfortable with adults.[30] Group composition changed according to the availability of children at the shelter.

The study questions were addressed in each group as the children used their photographs to discuss what was special to them. The first interview with the children was used to describe the study, explain the use of the cameras, distribute them and discuss the meaning of the word, special. The purpose of the second interview was to enable the children to view their photographs, discuss them with the group and select their five most special pictures. The third interview was used to give the children their enlarged special photographs. The children ranked these photos from the least special to most special and discussed them with the investigator.

Photography

Cameras and photographs were essential instruments for this study. The Polaroid Sidekick 35 mm Camera with flash was used. This is a disposable automatic focus camera with a built in flash. The Polaroid camera was chosen because of the quality of the finished pictures, the technical simplicity of operation, and economics. The camera had 27 exposures and the children were instructed to use all of the film. The investigator gave the child-participants individual disposable cameras.

The cameras were taken to a lab for film processing. The photographs were processed and duplicates were made of each picture. The investigator gave one copy of the photographs to the children and one copy was kept by the investigator for data analysis. The child-participants were given small photograph albums in which to keep their photographs when the study was completed. The photograph albums held 32 photos. The children's five selected special pictures were enlarged to 5 x 7 photographs. The purpose of enlarging the photographs was twofold. First, it aided in the identification of the special pictures throughout the third interview. This was particularly important due to the inherent confusion in a small groom with three children and approximately 60 photographs. Secondly, enlarging the special photographs facilitated the child-participant's discussion of the pictures. It was easier for the child-participants to focus on their special pictures because of their enlargement in size. Additionally, as one of the child-participants observed "we could see them better."

DATA MANAGEMENT AND ANALYSIS

Data were analyzed as it was generated in the form of transcripts, photographs, and field notes. The first step in heuristic data analysis is gathering all of the data from one participant and becoming immersed in the data until it is fully understood.[31] The transcripts were separated from group interview sessions into individual child-participant transcripts. The photographs for each child-participant were simultaneously reviewed with the transcripts of the interviews. Transcript statements were compared to individual photographs to ascertain the child-participant's meaning in the photograph. The heuristic process of immersion led to a gradual illumination as themes emerged from the data. The investigator reflected on the data from each child-participant until a clear depiction of what was special for that child was revealed. A portrait of the child-participant's experience of special was constructed. This portrait contained all of the qualities and themes that encompassed the child-participant's experience. Once the portrait was completed the investigator returned to the data to assess whether the portrait fit the data. When there was a clear depiction of the themes essential to the child's experience, the investigator began the immersion process again with the data from the next child participant. The data from each child-participant were developed into a portrait reflecting the patterns and themes portrayed by each child. Then all of the individual depictions were gathered together and the researcher searched for universal themes.[32] A composite depiction was developed into a portrait representing the group experience. The last step of heuristic data management is a creative synthesis of the experience. In characterizing the phenomena the investigator drew on all of the experiences of the research quest including data from interview sessions, field notes and the reflective journal to "create an aesthetic rendition of the themes and essential meanings of the phenomenon."[33]

TRUSTWORTHINESS

When a heuristic method is used, data is gathered from participants using unstructured conversational interviews. The concept of trustworthiness in heuristic research is one of meaning.[34] Through exhaustive self-searching, rigorous immersion and living through the phenomenon, depictions of the essence of the experience emerge. The investigator is the only one who has lived and become this process from engagement through incubation, immersion, illumination, explication, and creative synthesis. Moustakas states "the judgement of validity is made by the primary researcher."[35] There are no rules to guide trustworthiness, but returning again and again to the data enables the investigator to check the depictions that have emerged. It is necessary to determine if the themes and essences extracted are credible. A return to the participants with the composite descriptions will establish credibility, acknowledging this may be difficult as families living in homeless shelters tend to move frequently. Another method of establishing trustworthiness is publishing the results.[36] In publishing, the investigator takes responsibility for the analysis of the phenomenon. The reaction and response of readers to the study may determine whether the essence of the experience has been elucidated.

Qualitative researchers must develop their own criteria to establish the goodness of research. According to Marshall, "Good research comes from good method properly applied . . . good research is honest, open inquiry where the researcher searches for alternative explanations and is self-critical.[37]

NOTES

1. Watson, J. (1989). "Human caring and suffering: A subjective model for health sciences." In R. Taylor & J. Watson (Eds.). *They Shall Not Hurt, Human Suffering and Human Caring*. Boulder, CO: Colorado Associated University Press.
2. Faux, S.A., Walsh, M., & Deatrick, J.A. (1988). "Intensive interviewing of children and adolescents." *Western Journal of Nursing Research*, 10(2), 180-193.
3. Faux, et al., see note 2 above.
4. Faux, et al., see note 2 above.
5. Watson, J. (1988). *Nursing: Human Science and Human Care*. New York: National League for Nursing.
6. Moustakas, C. (1990). *Heuristic Research*. Newbury, CA: Sage Publications.
7. Watson, see note 5 above.
8. Talento, B. (1990). "Jean Watson." In J. George (Ed.), *Nursing Theories: The Base for Professional Nursing Practice*. Norwalk, CN: Appleton & Lange.
9. Moustakas, see note 6 above.
10. Moustakas, see note 6 above.
11. Moustakas, C. (1961). *Loneliness*. Englewood Cliffs, NY: Prentice-Hall.
12. Douglas, B.G. & Moustakas, C. (1985). "Heuristic inquiry: The internal search to know." *Journal of Humanistic Psychology*, 25(3), 39-55.
13. Moustakas, see note 6 above.
14. Douglass & Moustakas, see note 12 above.
15. Moustakas, see note 6 above.
16. Moustakas, see note 6 above.
17. Moustakas, see note 6 above.
18. Bernthal, N.I. (1990). "Motherhood lost and found: The experience of becoming an adoptive mother to a foreign-born child." (Doctoral dissertation, The Union). *University Microfilms International*.
19. Clarke, P., Williams, C. Percy, M., & Kim. Y. (1995). "Health and life problems of homeless men and women in the southeast." *Journal of Community Health Nursing*, 12(2), 101-110.
20. Moustakas, see note 6 above.
21. Parse, R.R. (1987). *Nursing Science*. Phila., PA: W.B. Saunders Company.
22. Moustakas, see note 6 above.
23. Moustakas, see note 6 above.
24. Snyder, R. (1988). "The experience of rejecting love." (Doctoral dissertation, the Union). *University Microfilms International*.

25. Bernthal, see note 18 above.

26. Bernthal, see note 18 above.

27. Snyder, see note 24 above.

28. Landreth, G. (1991). *Play Therapy: The Art of the Relationship.* Munice, IN: Accelerated Development Inc. Publishers.

29. Landreth, see note 28 above.

30. Malchiodi, C. (1990). *Breaking the Silence, Art Therapy with Children From Violent Homes.* NY: Bruner/Maxel Publishers.

31. Moustakas, C. (1967). "Heuristic research." In J.F.T. Bugental (Ed.). *Challenges of Humanistic Psychology.* NY: McGraw-Hill.

32. Moustakas, see note 6 above.

33. Moustakas, see note 6 above.

34. Moustakas, see note 6 above.

35. Moustakas, see note 6 above.

36. Moustakas, see note 6 above.

37. Marshall, C. (1990). "Goodness criteria: Are they objective or judgement calls?" In E.G. Guba (Ed.), *The Paradigm Dialog.* CA: Sage Publications, Inc.

IV

Special Things

In this chapter the data obtained from the study are presented. This chapter is divided into sections including the descriptions of the child participants, photographic analysis, a thematic analysis and the creative synthesis. The child-participants are not identified by their real names to protect their confidentiality.

THE CHILD PARTICIPANTS

Twelve children were included in the study. They ranged in age form 6 to 12 years, with an average of 8.6 years. There were 8 girls and 4 boys. Five of the children were European-American and 7 were African-American. Three sibling groups were involved, one family had 3 children in the study and two other families had 2 each. Six children were staying at the shelter with their mothers, 2 children were with their fathers and 4 children were with both parents. Seven children had been at the shelter for less than one week. Three children had been at the shelter for one week, and two had been there longer than a month. All of the children said this was their first homeless experience. Eleven of the child-participants were in their correct grade level for their age, and one child was a year behind. They attended a local public school. Demographic data are included in Table III. The average age of the child-participants was 9 years old.

Table III Demographic Data Categories	# of children	% of total
Age:	N=12	
6 years old	4	33%
7 years old	1	8%
9 years old	2	17%
10 years old	3	25%
12 years old	2	17%
Number of Siblings		
0	3	25%
1	3	25%
2	5	42%
3 or more	1	8%
Grade Level		
Kindergarten	4	33%
1st Grade	1	8%
3rd Grade	2	17%
4th Grade	3	25%
6th Grade	2	17%

Descriptions of Child-Participants

Kelly was a 12 year old girl. She had been at the shelter for one week. Kelly's family included her mother, step-father, step-brother (Jason) and step-sister (Elizabeth). They had come to the shelter together. Kelly's mother and new step-father had moved the family from their home in Delaware to be near the step-father's aging parents. Before arriving at the family shelter, they had stayed in a motel, and then in a:

> . . . military place, they had to
> separate the men from the children
> and we had this room with other
> people, we didn't like it, it was really
> a bad place.

Kelly's mother had been married 3 times. Kelly's father lived in Delaware, as did the father of her brother and sister. Kelly's new step-father had married their mother one year ago. Kelly hadn't told anyone at school where she was staying because:

> . . . people get the wrong idea, like you're poor, but you got to have a place to stay if you're going to get a job, you can't always stay in hotels.

Kelly described the shelter as a:

> place to call home, people care about you.

Kelly was a bright, bubbly adolescent with shoulder length, sandy-colored hair. She was very talkative, and frequently monopolized the conversation in the group. Kelly was quick to smile and laugh, but avoided eye contact with her step sister Elizabeth, who was also in the group. In just a week, Kelly reported that she had formed friendships with the other children, and found at least one "boyfriend." She liked:

> acting crazy with my friends.

Kelly's photographs did not include any pictures of her family. Her most special picture was a picture of a blanket with a football insignia on it.

Kelly Top 5 Special Pictures	Rank
Raiders blanket	1
the shelter	2
younger friends	3
friends and boyfriend	4
friends	5

Elizabeth was 10 years old. She was Kelly's half-sister. Elizabeth had long brown hair and dark brown eyes. During the interview Elizabeth sat quietly in a chair (the other children sat on the floor), and only spoke when asked a direct question. Included in her pictures were photographs of flowers growing at the shelter. Elizabeth did not take any pictures of her parents. However, when asked if she could take another picture what would it be, she replied that she would have liked to have a picture of her mother. Elizabeth said:

> My mommy, because she is special
> and she had me and she'll be with me
> for the rest of my life . . . and my real
> dad, because I love him and he loves
> me too, and I don't get to see him a
> lot.

Elizabeth's most special picture was a picture of herself:

> The first picture is a picture of me and
> I think that it's special because if I
> wasn't here then I wouldn't be as
> special as I am.

Pictures of her family were among her selected special photos:

> . . . and the second most special is my
> sister because since I was born she's
> been here my whole life, and my
> brother because he's my only brother.

The shelter was important to her because:

> I like being in a house.

A photograph of her clothing was her last special picture.

Elizabeth Top 5 Special Pictures	Rank
self	1
step-sister	2
brother	3
shelter	4
clothes	5

Daniel was 9 years old. He was Elizabeth's brother and Kelly's half-brother. Daniel had dark hair and eyes like his sister. He had tremendous energy, even for a nine year old boy. There were not many boys at the shelter his age, but he found a "best friend" in Jason (six years old). Daniel was the only child-participant who took pictures at both the shelter and school. He took a picture of his whole class because:

> When I like find a house and I'm out of
> school, I will forget what they look
> like and what their names were, I still
> remember some.

Daniel also took a picture of his step-father:

> so I'll remember him if he ever moves
> out.

When asked if that was a possibility he said:

> well, you never know.

Daniel reported that:

> my   step-father   is   mean   to   me
> sometimes,   he   yells,   my   mom
> understands me better.

Daniel could not stay seated in his chair, despite repeated encouragement
from the investigator. Daniel moved around the room, touching every
object and opening every drawer and cabinet. He had to be reminded to
discuss his photographs, instead of playing with Jason, or wandering
around the room. His most special picture was a picture of his "best
friend," Jason.

Daniel Top 5 Special Pictures	Rank
"best friend" Jason	1
teacher	2
class at school	3
school friend	4
playground slide	5

Tina was 12 years old and an only child. She was tall for her age
and thin. Tina and her mom came to the shelter after staying with
relatives for a period of time. The shelter was in the same school
district as her old house, so she didn't change schools. All of Tina's
pictures were taken at school. Tina didn't take a picture of her mother,
she explained:

> I was so excited, I couldn't wait til the
> next morning to go to school, I just
> ran my film out, I just ran out of film,
> I just forgot about my momma . . . I
> wanted to take a picture of her cause
> she will be with me her whole life.

Tina was very reserved in the beginning. Initially she wouldn't speak unless asked a direct question. She made only occasional and brief eye contact. After the first round of questions was completed, she began to spontaneously offer her comments and ideas. By the end of the interview she was laughing and smiling. The other children laughed at the funny descriptions she gave of her pictures. The more the children laughed the more excited Tina became, using her hands to express herself, making silly faces, laughing and acting out scenes from her pictures. A picture of herself was her most special picture:

> My most special picture is this little
> girl, and her name is Tina. The reason
> why I say she is so special is because
> we go places together, and it's like we
> have the same mind and everyone
> says she dresses like me and we dress
> alike, we do a lot of things together
> and I can say things and she won't go
> back and say 'em. I really enjoy being
> around her and she won't go back and
> say 'em. I really enjoy being around
> her.

Tina's other special pictures were of her friends.

> Friends are very important, they make
> me laugh, I like that, and when you
> laugh you forget your troubles.

Tina Top 5 Special Pictures	Rank
self	1
school friends	2
best friends	3
school friends	4
self with school friends	5

Katie was 9 years old with deep dimples and long blonde hair. She laughed and giggled during the interview. Katie was the oldest of three children. They had arrived at the shelter with their father. Katie's mother was in another state. Katie stated that she "misses my mom." It wasn't until the last interview that Katie confided that her mother was in jail. Katie had said that her mother was:

> working in another state, and it may
> be a long time before my mom gets
> transferred up here.

Except when talking about her mother, Katie made jokes, laughed with the other children, and made frequent eye contact with the investigator. When Katie mentioned her mother she became very serious, stopped telling jokes, sat motionless and didn't smile. Katie volunteered that:

> I learned a lot from my mom even though she quit in 9th grade . . . she quit in 9th grade, got pregnant and then went back to school, so she quit, went back, quit, went back she was like in and out of school, but she taught me a lot about school, that's why I love school.

Katie said some of her friends at school have stayed at the shelter before, but:

> The 4th and 5th graders pick on me, but I don't worry about it, at least they're happy cause it ain't them, but I'm getting a house.

Katie's most special picture was a picture of herself, followed by another picture of herself.

Katie Top 5 Special Pictures	Rank
Grandmother	1
Wolverine toy	2
best friend	3
friend and best friend	4
friends	5

Nelson was 10 years old, tall and thin with large brown eyes. He wore glasses. He had been at the shelter with his mother for two months. Nelson was an only child. He was very quiet and reserved. During the interviews, he did not speak unless asked a direct question, and when the other children were laughing he would only smile. Though quiet Nelson was cooperative and gave thoughtful answers to questions. When asked during the initial interview to describe a special toy he replied:

> it would have gears, wheels that help
> the toy to move because batteries can
> help it move and sometimes the
> battery would be dead. If it had gears,
> it can move by itself

Nelson said that he was ready to leave the shelter and find:

> a nice place that's clean and have a lot
> of rooms that you can sleep in and a
> refrigerator that you can put your food
> in.

Nelson Top 5 Special Pictures	Rank
mother	1
friend's mother	2
friend	3
investigator	4
self	5

Nikki was 9 years old. She had large brown eyes and black hair divided into several small braids on her head. Nikki was at the shelter with her mother. She was the youngest of six children. Her siblings were staying with their grandmother. Nikki had lived at the shelter for over a month. She said:

> it's okay here, there's always
> someone to play with.

Nikki was small for her age and very thin. Her mother volunteered that "she had a heart defect at birth and had several open heart surgeries, last time the heart doctor checked her she was fine." Nikki was outgoing and sociable. Whenever the investigator arrived at the shelter, Nikki was always at the center of a group of children. The other little girls wanted to be interviewed in the same group as Nikki. During the interviews Nikki was talkative, but sat quietly while the other children described their pictures. Nikki's most special pictures included a picture of a young friend who was about 2 years old:

> I call her 'big cheeks' cause her cheeks
> are so fat, she is cute.

Nikki Top 5 Special Pictures	Rank
mother	1
self	2
friends	3
younger friends	4
friends	5

Antwan was 7 years old. He was a thin child, about average height for his age. While he smiled readily when discussing his pictures, he didn't laugh and play as much as the other children. He was the only boy in his family, with two younger sisters. They had come to the shelter with their mother about a week ago. Antwan and his family had moved several times in the last few months. He like the shelter the best of all the places they lived because:

> we didn't have anything to play with
> before we came here.

Antwan took multiple pictures of his mother and two younger sisters. He also took pictures of:

> everything that we brought from
> home.

Antwan's most special picture was a picture of his mother:

> because she loves us and that's all.

Antwan Top 5 Special Pictures	Rank
mother	1
self	2
friend	3
sister and friend	4
investigator	5

Whitney was Antwan's sister. She was 6 years old. Whitney had big brown eyes, black hair and dimples when she smiled. She was literally jumping up and down with excitement about seeing her pictures. Once she was given the pictures she sat down on the floor and carefully examined each one. She had brought her "doll babies" from home. Whitney was very concrete in her descriptions of her photographs:

This is a picture of a house, this is my
mom, these are my baby dolls.

The majority of her pictures were focused on her mother, brother and
younger sister.

Whitney Top 5 Special Pictures	Rank
mother	1
friend	2
shelter	3
self	4
investigator	5

Lakisha was also 6 years old. Lakisha came to the shelter with her
mother and father. She was an only child. Lakisha's black hair was
braided and piled on top of her head. Of the three 6 year old girls,
Lakisha was the quietest. She waited patiently for her turn, sitting on
the floor watching the other children. She answered all of the questions
asked of her and eventually volunteered information as well. Lakisha's
most special picture was a picture of her mother and father embracing in
a doorway.

Lakisha Top 5 Special Pictures	Rank
mom and dad	1
mother	2
self	3
friend	4
investigator	5

Angela was also an only child. She was 6 years old. Angela was
tall, with a very round face and large brown eyes. Angela and her
mother arrived at the shelter several days before the interview. After
watching the older children taking pictures for the study, Angela was so
excited about taking her pictures that she said:

I couldn't sleep last night.

She took all of the pictures as soon as she was given the camera.
Angela tried several times to take a picture of the moon. She said
simply that:

I love the moon.

Unfortunately, the pictures were not successful and it was difficult to see the moon in them. Angela said:

> I really wanted a picture of the moon,

and then picked up the other pictures and began describing them. Angela said that she:

> loves babies, because they're pretty

She took a picture of the baby at the shelter. The telephone was a very important object for Angela:

> cause I like to talk to Grandma and
> one of my friends

Angela's most special picture was a picture of the telephone.

Angela Top 5 Special Photographs	Rank
telephone	1
friend's room	2
friend's room	3
shelter	4
younger friend	5

PHOTOGRAPHIC ANALYSIS

During the interview sessions the child-participants reviewed and discussed their photographs with the investigator. The questions on the interview guide were used to focus the interview sessions. Specifically, the child participants were asked to describe their pictures and explain why they were special. The youngest children explained their photographs in very concrete terms, which was developmentally appropriate for their age. The older children expressed more emotions, linked their photographs to other experiences and tended to digress into related topics. The detailed level of their descriptions was also characteristic of children in this age group who are beginning to think abstractly.

The child-participants' descriptions of their photographs were accepted and used as data whether the children gave detailed accounts of their photographs and were analyzed concurrently with the content of the photographs. The ranking of the photographs were also considered a factor in the analysis. The second research question addressed by this study determined the feasibility of using photographs as a data generating technique with children. All of the children were able to take photographs that portrayed what was special to them, and then were able to give a description of their photographs to the investigator.

The Photographs

Of the 324 possible photographs, 272 (84%) were returned from the developer. Of the 27 pictures taken by each child-participant an average of 23 were successfully processed. One child-participant received 27 of her photographs and one received only 15 (although she made two attempts). As indicated in Table IV, the photographs were analyzed and themes were derived from the children's descriptions of the content of the photographs (i.e. "this is a picture of my stuffed bear, I've had it since I was a baby").

Table IV Photographic Themes Themes	# of photographs	% of total
things from home	18	7%
shelter	33	12%
self	35	13%
adult friends	36	13%
family	48	18%
child friends	102	37%
Total	272	

Shelter

These photographs were generally taken outside in the shelter courtyard. The children focused their pictures on porches, the buildings, and the playground. This theme comprised 12% of the total pictures and 12% of the selected special pictures:

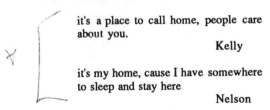

>   it's a place to call home, people care
>   about you.
>   Kelly
>
>   it's my home, cause I have somewhere
>   to sleep and stay here
>   Nelson

Adult Friends

This theme included photographs of non-relative, adult friends of the child-participants, either from the shelter or school. Adult friends accounted for 13% of the total pictures, 12% of the selected special photographs but none were included in the most special pictures:

> I like this one because I like Travis
> and he's my mom's best friend.
>   Nikki

> cause you're friendly and you're nice
>   Katie

Things From Home

This theme included objects brought from home such as photographs, favorite toys, and clothes. Things from home comprised 7% of the total pictures taken, 7% of the selected special pictures and 9% of the most special pictures. Kelly chose her Raiders blanket as her most special picture:

> My Raiders blanket, . . . it makes
> things happen, cause when you get
> under it makes you warm.
>   Kelly

Child-friends

Pictures of friends accounted for 37% of the total number of photographs, 36% of the selected special photographs, and 9% of the most special pictures. Child friends were frequently ranked as the third, fourth or fifth selected special pictures:

> I like him cause he's crazy and he can
> tell this stuff to make me laugh like if
> I'm sad
>   Kelly

> These are my best friends, I can trust
> them.
>   Tina

> All my friends are special to me so I
> took pictures of them to remember
> them and how they act.
>   Katie

Daniel selected a picture of his "best friend" as his most special picture:

> . . . cause he's my best friend, and he
> always will be.
>   Daniel

Self

Several children experimented with self-photography. They held the camera at arms length and then took the picture. Other children asked friends, parents or other adults to take pictures of them. Pictures of the child-participants comprised 13% of the total pictures, 15% of the selected special pictures, and 27% of the most special pictures:

> This one makes me feel happy
> Nelson

> I don't know why I'm special to myself, I just am.
> Nikki

Family

These pictures included family members. Extended family members were sometimes represented by a telephone used to connect the family member with the child participant, or a toy given to the child by the absent family member. Family members comprised 18% of the total picture, 18% of the selected special pictures and 55% of the most special pictures. Jason chose his "granny" as his most special picture. Lakisha's most special picture was a picture of her mother and father together. Nikki, Nelson, Antwan and Whitney described a picture of their mother as their most special picture:

> Cause I love her, and that's all
> Nelson

Five Selected Special Photographs

The child-participants were asked to select the five pictures that were the most special to them of all their photographs. These pictures were enlarged to 5 x 7 prints. The most special photographs are indicated in Table V. Themes developed from the initial interview sessions were used throughout the analysis. As the children selected their 5 special photographs they were encouraged to discuss their pictures in greater depth than they had previously. Some of the children repeated their earlier descriptions but most of the child-participants added details to their previous descriptions.

Table V Themes	# of photographs	% of total
things from home	4	7%
shelter	7	12%
self	9	15%
adult friends	7	12%
family	11	18%
child friends	22	36%
Total	60	

Most Special Photograph

The children were asked to rank their top five pictures from the most to the least special. Once again they were asked to describe their pictures and say why they were special. They were also asked to explain why they placed their photographs in that order. Only one of the child-participants asked, "didn't I already do that last night?" The researcher replied, "yes you did, but I am hoping that you will tell me even more about your pictures tonight." One of the youngest child-participants was unable to rank her pictures, or even select a favorite picture. The other children did not have any difficulty ranking their pictures. Six children selected a picture of a family member as their most special picture, three chose pictures of themselves, one selected a friend, and one chose a picture of a favorite object as indicated in Table VI. The themes of shelter and adult friends did not appear in the most special pictures.

Table VI Most Special Photograph Themes	# of photographs	% of total
things from home	1	9%
child friends	1	9%
self	3	27%
family	6	55%
Total	11	

THEMATIC ANALYSIS

Themes emerged from written transcripts and photograph. They were analyzed in accordance with Moustakas' heuristic method. As each child-participants' data was entered, comprehensively reviewed and analyzed core themes were recorded. When all of the data from each child-participant had been fully understood the themes from each child-participant were considered as a whole. Themes derived individually were analyzed together and patterns which unified the group experience were identified. These patterns were developed into themes which expressed the essence of what was special to the child-participants.

The themes which emerged differed according to the ages of the child-participants. Themes which were significant to children between the ages of 6 and 7 years were different from the themes which emerged from the data of the children ages 9 to 12 years old. For simplicity these groups will be labeled school age (6-7 year olds) and pre-adolescents (ages 9-12 years) and are presented separately for each age group.

School-age Children

Two themes emerged from the school age children's data. These were labeled "having fun", and "special people." The theme "having fun" arose from initial themes of the shelter, things from home, child and adult friends. The children emphasized the enjoyment they were having at the time. One child took a picture of a special toy:

> That's Wolverine . . . he's a
> X-Man . . . he's a good guy . . . he can
> fight and stick people . . . he's fun

Two children had a picture of the shelter among their special selected pictures:

> It's fun here...you don't have to pay
> no money for food.
>
> Jason

> It's really nice here... we didn't have
> anything to play with before we came
> here.
>
> Antwan

A picture of the investigator was placed fifth by three of the children:

> You can sneak in the house at night
> and give us candy.
>
> Whitney

> You can get us out of bed and take us
> to Disney World.
>
> Lakisha

> You're special cause you did this and it
> was fun.
>> Antwan

One child placed a picture of a friend fifth. The other children ranked pictures of their friends second, third, or fourth:

> Cause they are my friends . . . friends
> play with you.
>> Jason

> That's my friend, too . . . friends play
> together.
>> Antwan

The second theme to emerge from this data was "special people." Four of the five child-participants in this age group selected a most favorite picture from their five special pictures. Of these four, one chose a picture of his grandmother as the most special, and three chose a picture of their mother as their most special picture:

> My granny . . . she buys us candy . . .
> she takes care of us, but she is always
> picking on my pa.
>> Jason

> My mom is the most special . . . she
> takes care of me . . . she loves us.
>> Antwan

> My mom, cause she's pretty.
>> Whitney

> My most special picture is of my
> mom and dad . . . cause they love me.
>> Lakisha

Being with special people was extremely important to the child participants as evidenced by the ranking of these pictures as their most special picture.

Pre-adolescents

There were seven child-participants in this age group. These children were more expressive verbally than the younger children. Two themes emerged; "feeling cared for" and "always there."

"Feeling cared for" reflected valued relationships the children established with peers and adult friends. The theme "feeling cared for" encompassed the subthemes of "belonging", "trusting" and "relieving stress." Friendships were an integral part of the theme "belonging":

> We're like sisters at school . . . she
> tells me things and I tell her things.
>
> Kelly

> My friends at school are really
> important to me, and if I didn't take a
> picture of my class they would have
> been really upset, and I would've too.
>
> Jason

> I like this because he's my friend
> I like this because I like them both.
>
> Nelson

> He's my friend, he's my friend, he's
> my friend and he's my friend and
> here's another group of friends, here,
> here, and here. Lot's of friends, isn't
> it?
>
> Daniel

Most of the child-participants reported they didn't tell anyone at school they were homeless, for fear of being teased. Even the two children who continued to attend the same school did not tell their friends. Several of the child-participants did tell friends they were staying at the shelter but they said it didn't matter to their friends:

> They didn't say anything.
>
> Elizabeth

> They said 'so what'?
>
> Daniel

Katie said her friends didn't care because many of them had also been at a shelter except:

> The 4th and 5th graders pick on me
> but I don't worry about it at least
> they're happy cause it ain't them, but
> I'm getting a house.
>
> Katie

"Trust" was the quality that differentiated friends from "best friends." Three of the participants described their "best friends" as someone who could be trusted:

> These are my best friends, I can trust them . . . they make me laugh, I like that . . . they all treat me like cousins. They treat me real nice and stuff . . . they take me places and we go places together . . . other friends you can be their friend one day and one day they won't be your friend, like if you tell them something, they will go back and tell another person-that's not a real friend.

"Relieving stress" happened when people either helped the child-participants or they were laughing and having fun. Adult friends were mentioned in this subtheme when they were viewed as helpful to the children. One child included a teacher, one included the shelter manager, and one included the investigator in their selected special photographs:

> Monica, she's my best adult friend, she's one who cooks and she helps.
> > Katie

> My teacher, she is there most of the time and she helps a lot and if it wasn't for her I wouldn't have an education.
> > Nikki

"Relieving stress" for these child participants, involved playing and having fun:

> I like him cause he's crazy and he can tell this stuff to make me laugh like if I'm sad . . . they make me laugh when I'm down.
> > Tina

> Cause they're crazy and they look funny and they are more understanding . . . when they're acting normal they feel the pressure . . . he doesn't usually have a flower in his mouth.
> > Kelly

Family members were frequently photographed by the children. The children described "feeling cared for" by these family members. Only parents and siblings were present at the shelter with the children:

> my mom, because if she hadn't had me
> I wouldn't be here, and she teaches me
> right from wrong.
>
> Kelly

> my mom, my dad, my grandparents
> . . . cause they take care of me
> Katie

> if it wasn't for them (my brother and
> sisters) people would pick on me all
> the time
> Nikki

"Feeling care for" was directly related to being at the shelter. The child-participants took many pictures of the shelter. Only two children placed a picture of the shelter among their most special selected pictures:

> they're all like family, because they
> all care about you . . . and most
> people don't really care.
>
> Kelly

The theme "always there" emerged from the child-participants' description of their selected special photographs. Someone or something that was consistently available to provide affection and support for the participant was described as "always there." One child participant described an object from home as something that was always with her:

> My magical Raiders blanket, because
> I love my Raiders blanket . . .
> wherever I go stay it goes with me it
> makes things happen . . . if you tell it
> something, it can't tell anything else
> and if you tell it something you want
> to come true, it will come true. It
> does, it makes things come true.
>
> Kelly

Three child-participants described themselves as someone who was "always there":

cause that person (self) will always be
there when I need that person, myself
is there when I need them, when I'm
going crazy.

> Elizabeth

this one is of me and it's special cause
what's special about me is cause I like
myself, and it's a picture of me and I
really like myself

> Katie

she's my best friend (picture of
myself) of all because I can tell her
things and she won't go back and tell
and I can do things with her

> Tina

One child described her "best friend" as being "always there," and one
child-participant described his substitute teacher:

that's my best friend, I can depend on
her.

> Tina

and this one cause it's my teacher . . .
he's really nice and he's always there.
He's there every day.

> Daniel

Three of the child-participants referred to a family member who was
"always there for them":

cause she made me and she's been
through all my problems and we both
had hard times

> Nikki

My mother is, but it's nothing I can
say that anything else that I can think
is as special as her . . . cause she will
be with me, and I gonna say not all of
my life cause she gonna go, but she
will be with me as far as she could,
and she brought me into this world ...
she's the only thing I need.

> Tina

and the second most special is my
sister because since I was born she's
been here my whole life and my
brother because he is my most special
brother and he's my only brother.

Elizabeth

My mother, she's special and she had
me and she'll be with me for the rest
of my life.

Elizabeth

Additional Analysis

The previous themes were derived from interviews conducted with
the children about their photographs. During the interviews
conversations occurred spontaneously with the children which were not
directly related to the study question. Themes derived from those
conversations are included here, although not part of the photographs
these themes were important enough to the children to have been
recurring topics discussed during the interviews.

The theme "caring community" was defined as the environment
within the shelter walls that made the shelter more than a group of
buildings. The sense of being in a "caring community" was defined as
the environment within the shelter walls that made the shelter more
than a group of buildings. The sense of being in a "caring community"
was evident from the photographs of residents sitting together on the
porch, to the descriptions of the shelter by the children. During the
course of the data collection, an emergency occurred with a family and
the parents were unable to care for their children for a period of two
days. The other residents cared for the children, until the parent was able
to return. There was a strong feeling of being in a small village, where
everyone was dependent and relied on everyone else:

They're all like family, because they
all care about you.

Kelly

It's a place to call home, people care
about you.

Katie

It's fun here.

Jason

Several of the children said the shelter was special because "they
could eat there". It was generally the younger children who spoke about
the shelter providing "basic needs"

Don't have to pay no money for food.

Jason

My home cause I have somewhere to
sleep and stay.

Nelson

We didn't have anything to play with
before.

Antwan

Cause you can eat . . .

Lakisha

It's a home cause I have a place to live
in.

Angela

The themes "caring community encompassed the subtheme "basic
needs." The social and psychological elements that comprised the
experience of being in a caring community included having basic needs
met. Meeting the basic needs of food, and shelter is desperately
important for people who have lost their home. The two elements of
caring community and basic needs were recurring themes in discussions
with the children.

Another theme developed from these conversations was "danger
outside." The shelter was located in an area of high crime and drug use.
A fence surrounded the shelter both literally and figuratively. The older
children described the danger they saw out on the street:

All the way down there, that's a
hooker owned street. They're just
hanging out on the streets cause
maybe they're selling drugs . . . I
don't go there no more cause curfew is
at 6 o'clock.

Tina

It's not for kids up there (previous
house in Georgia), all the drugs and
drinking and people up there who
snatch kids.

Katie

> We were walking down the street and a
> man in a car rolled down his window
> and asked if we were hookers. I said
> 'no, we're just going to the store' . . .
> We got home fast.
>
>   Kelly

The theme "danger outside" describes the children's sense that the streets were not safe for them. In contrast to life outside the fence, the families in the shelter formed a protective community. Each adult was involved in the life of each child.

Summary

The children were excited and enthusiastic about participating in the study. They willingly shared their thoughts and photographs. Soon after arriving at the shelter it was clear that every child between the ages of 6 and 12 years would have to be included. The children crowded around as if I were Santa Claus with new toys for them. Even the parents were excited. There was a very festive feeling as children ran everywhere taking pictures. The entire shelter community was involved in the project. All of the residents were present at the last residents' meeting when the photo was presented.

The difference in the ages of the child-participants made it necessary to divide them into two different age groups for analysis. The younger children were primarily concerned with "having fun" and being with "special people." The older children described "feeling care for" and someone who was "always there" as the two issues which were the most special to them. The components of "feeling cared for" included "trusting," "belonging" and "relieving stress." The child-participants were able to take picture of what was special to these children. The child-participants were clearly able to describe the essence of what was most special to them. Additional analysis performed on the data gathered during informal conversations revealed the themes of "caring community" and "danger outside." This combination of interviews and photographs produced a synergistic effect that neither method could have elicited alone. Previous studies have used quantitative and qualitative interview methods to conduct research with children who are homeless. These methods each miss an important dimension. The photographs stimulated discussions as the children become expert witnesses and described their photographs. Even shy children were willing to share their thoughts and feelings when the photos were revealed. Analysis of the transcripts with the photographs helped the researcher to understand what was special to the children. Understanding what is special to children is enriched by placing it within the context of other life experiences.

V

Discussion and Future Research

This research study contributes significantly to the literature on homeless children by approaching the issue from the child's perspective. This study built on Heusel's study of *The Experience of Homelessness Viewed Through the Eyes of Homeless School-Age Children* by using photography to facilitate communication with children.[1] It also built on Hubbard's work with homeless children portrayed in *Shooting Back, A Photographic View of Life by Homeless Children* by adding interviews and qualitative analysis to the photography of children.[2] Hubbard's comments about the children that he worked with illustrate the findings of his study:

> I realized the love and protectiveness they had for each other. These children are so lovable and so vulnerable. They have witnessed and experienced so many horrors; they have been deprived of our society's riches. Yet despite deprivation and abandonment the children embody love, joy, strength and beauty. They are priceless.[3]

It is this love, joy, strength and beauty which must be uncovered to reveal a complete picture of the children behind the label "homeless." Knowledge of what brings love, joy, strength and beauty to homeless children can provide guidance for adults seeking to provide them with emotional support. The presence of caring adults in homeless shelters can help to "reduce the stress that can be reduced and support children through and after the part of the stress that is an inevitable aspect of life."[4]

The essential question of this research was "how do children who are homeless describe and portray what is special to them?" How the children became homeless; the problems they have encountered; how stressful is the homeless experience; these questions were not a part of this study. It is important to mention the latter because the majority of the research on homeless people (children and families) is focused on issues involving the difficult aspects of homelessness. The purpose of this study was not to underscore or negate the difficult aspects of homelessness for children, but to listen to the children as they described and portrayed what was special to them.

As described in previous research studies, the majority of the children were staying at the shelter with their mother and one or two siblings.[5] Several of the families had stayed with relatives prior to entering the shelter, one had moved from out of state looking for work, and one family had a history of drug abuse. These life situations prior to the occurrence of homelessness are similar to family situations reported in the literature on homelessness.[6]

The children who participated in this study were not assessed for health problems, psychological distress or learning disabilities. These are all important issues for homeless children as reported by Bassuk & Rubin, and Davidhizer & Frank.[7] Eleven out of 12 of the children were working at their grade level in school, although previous studies have documented school failure as a significant issue for homeless children.[8]

Heusel's qualitative study of the school-age child's experience of homelessness described positive experiences such as maintaining a loving relationship with parents, making new friends, feeling safe and having room to play.[9] The experiences of the children in Heusel's study were similar to those of the children in the present study. In describing what was special to them, the children included their parents, making new friends, feeling cared for and having fun. Both Heusel's study and the present study were unusual in the literature on homeless children because they reveal positive experiences which are possible for these children.

An important consideration in the interpretation of the results of the present study was the homeless shelter where the research was conducted. There are multiple agencies involved in providing for the homeless. Accommodations, assistance and safety vary from shelter to shelter. According to Bassuk & Gallagher, homeless shelters as opposed to homeless hotels, may provide enough support to mitigate some of the difficult aspects of homeless life for children.[10] The present study was conducted in a family shelter. A full-time social worker provided case-management, there was an after-school program and a daycare program. The physical design of the shelter was compatible with establishing a social network. The buildings were arranged facing a courtyard which included a basketball court, and a playground. The buildings had large front porches where the residents and children could congregate after dinner. Residents of the shelter would sit or stand on the porch and talk while the children played in the courtyard. This opportunity for adults to form supportive networks cultivated a feeling of community. Homeless shelters which provide opportunities for children to develop supportive relationships can contribute significantly to minimizing the disruption and disequilibrium inherent in the homeless experience. Children who believe there is a place where people will care for them will learn to be hopeful in the face of adversity.[11] They physical attributes of the shelter were conducive to the development of friendships between peers and children and adults. The study results may have been very different in a homeless hotel where families are isolated from each other.

A close relationship between peers can minimize some of the destructive aspects of being homeless.[12] Friendships were certainly important to the child-participants in this study as 50% of the total pictures were either of adult friends or of peers. The ability to seek out peer friendships is an important aspect of development in the school-aged years.[13] The need to separate from parents and independently form relationships is increasingly important between the ages of 7-12 years. Additionally, children who are resilient in the face of adversity are able to seek out a network of friends and relatives can provide support.[14] Providing opportunities in shelters for children to play and interact with children and other adults is crucial to their development. Siblings may turn to each other for nurturance and protection.[15] Their support can play a role in counteracting feelings of isolation and neglect.[16] The child-participants frequently took pictures of their siblings and described them as:

> this is a picture of my sister, and she
> has been with me since I was born.
> Elizabeth

Garmezy identified three factors which may influence a child's ability to be resilient in stressful circumstances.[17] These include: a) temperament factors; b) a warm, cohesive family or concerned family member; and c) external support networks such as teachers, coaches or the parents of friends. The child-participants frequently identified family members and adult friends as someone special. Thirty-one percent of the total pictures were taken of family members or adult friends.

Previous research studies warn of the detrimental influences of homelessness on children. More recently, research studies have focused on the strength and resiliency of children living in unusual circumstances.[18] The current study focused on what homeless children portray and describe as special in order to uncover the child's perspective. Understanding children's perspectives will aid the development of programs designed to mitigate the negative aspects of homelessness.

DISCUSSION

Jean Watson's conceptualization of Human Care was the orienting framework for this study. According to Watson, humans possess unique inner resources and strengths that can be drawn upon to meet health challenges.[19] This study was designed to uncover the unique inner resources and strengths of the children. The investigator's belief in Jean Watson's conceptualization of Human Care informed the selection and development of the study design and Interview Guide. The children's spontaneous photographs of the investigator and later placement of those pictures among the selected special photographs indicates a level of "shared humaneness."[20] The investigator participated in the lived reality of the children, and became an important element in the photographs. Within an atmosphere of caring and compassion, the children were able to share their feelings and thoughts, verbally and non-verbally. Through their use of photography and discussions, the children's meanings were revealed. Four major themes were uncovered. These were characterized as "having fun" and "special people" for the school-age children and "feeling cared for" and "always there" for the pre-adolescent child-participants.

Having Fun

The school-age children emphasized "having fun" or playing in their photographs and discussions. Play is the natural medium of self-expression in children of this age group. Through the process and content of their play, the children can release pent up feelings of anger and aggression, fears and anxiety. During play, children are able to regain a sense of equilibrium, as they strive to make sense of their world.[21] The children's preoccupation with play demonstrates developmentally appropriate behavior while offering an avenue for nursing programs to support and enhance the child's coping strategies.

Special People

Children look to their parents to protect and support them. When parents fail in their attempt, the children will seek out another adult to shield and nurture them.[22] "Special people" was an important theme. Photographs of "special people" included, parents, siblings, friends, adult friends, and babies. Stable shelter staff could contribute to the children's sense of security and provide parents with respite from the demands of child care. The strong sense of community at the shelter was reflected in Kelly's statement:

> they're all like family . . . cause they
> all care about you here.
>   Kelly

Feeling Cared For

"Feeling cared for" encompassed the subthemes of "belonging," "trusting" and "relieving stress." For a pre-adolescent, forming relationships with friends is an important developmental stage. The key psychosocial growth issues in this age group are separation and independence from family members, cognitive expansion, sexual identity, moral maturation and preparation for an adult role in society.[23] A sense of belonging is essential to children.[24] One of the fundamental tasks of growing up is to "find a place in a valued group that gives a sense of belonging . . . and to develop reliable and predictable relationships with other people, especially a few close friends and loved ones."[25] The children took many pictures of their friends.

"Trusting" was a theme which surfaced when the child-participants spoke of their "best friend." The element that differentiated a friend from a "best friend" was the ability to trust that person with secrets and important information. Trust is one of the primary aspects of any relationship. Frequently, it is a lack of trust which inhibits the development of adult support networks and may end in homelessness when limited resources are strained. Psychological trauma is described as the "rupture of interpersonal trust and the loss of a sense of personal control."[26] Fostering trusting relationships, and learning to trust may help prevent the intergenerational cycle of homelessness.

The child participants frequently mentioned their friends when they spoke of "relieving stress." They discussed laughing, acting crazy, "making me laugh when I'm down" as ways to "reduce the pressure." The stress of being homeless or living in a shelter is a traumatic event.[27] According to Luthar and Zigler, resilient, highly stressed children scored higher in humor generation than highly stressed less resilient children.[28] Laughing and having fun may provide a buffer against stress for these children.

Always There

The theme "always there" referred to an object or person which was always available for the child. Underneath this theme seemed to be a concern that no one would be there for the child. One child described a special blanket, one mentioned a friend of only four days, three children described themselves as the person could always rely on, and six named a family member. In the instability of shelter life, the semblance of permanence was sought. Many of the child-participants had moved recently from out of town, or out of state leaving friends and family behind. The desire to reconnect and establish bonds may reflect a need for nurturance and protection. The shelter staff can relieve some of the children's distress by providing structure, routine and supportive limit setting.[29]

Summary

The answer to the research question, "what do children who are homeless portray and describe as special?" is different for children in different age groups. For the younger children, the answer was playing and being with special people. For the older, pre-adolescent children, the answer was feeling cared for and having a stable relationship with significant others. A sense of safety, security and continuity is important in the establishment of an environment where children can explore relationships and create networks of friendship and family.

IMPLICATIONS FOR RESEARCH

The results of this study imply that research which focuses on the perspectives and understandings of children is needed. Gaining insight into the world of children will enable researchers to develop accurate theories about the meaning of events that occur during childhood. Children living in vulnerable situations are at risk. Research studies focusing on children and family strengths will guide the development of programs designed to foster growth despite family deprivation.

In the present study, the children were asked to describe what was "special" to them. Asking children to describe another word such as "important" or "valuable" may elicit different results, providing a more comprehensive view of the child's experience. This study could be replicated with children living in the inner-cities, rural settings, and suburban neighborhoods. Additionally, children from various ethnic backgrounds, traditional and non-traditional families, and children living in foster-homes may all provide unique perspectives of what is special to children.

The combination of qualitative interviews with an expressive arts method led to richer data than either method could have elicited alone. This is an especially valuable method for conducting research with children because of the problems inherent in interviewing children. Although this method could be used with virtually any population, continued development of this technique will enhance data collection from child-participants. Besides photography, video taping, drawings, story-telling, drama, poetry and even dance may be used in conjunction with the research interview.

Themes generated from this study would benefit from further investigation. Replicating this study at a larger shelter and/or a shelter with different design characteristics would be valuable. The physical

design of the shelter used in the present study may have contributed
significantly to the type of data generated. The three wide porches, low-
buildings, courtyard design, and small size (only 14-16 families)
facilitated community interaction. The parents typically sat on the
porches, talking and watching the children play. After-school programs,
day-care and a committed staff all add to the feeling of community.
Studies which could document outcomes from different types of shelters
would help direct public funding to those which provide the most
benefit for the residents.

While all of the children, except one, were at their appropriate grade
level in school, many of them had difficulty expressing their ideas
verbally to the investigator. Poor verbal skills hinder school
performance. Studies examining the particular areas of educational
difficulty among vulnerable children may produce results which can be
used to focus after-school activities to develop these areas. Giving
children cameras and asking them to talk about their pictures is just one
example of how children can be encouraged to exercise their verbal
skills Additionally, the use of an open-ended discussion of the children's
pictures could serve as a way of assessing verbal skills.

IMPLICATIONS FOR NURSING PRACTICE

Research studies which generate nursing theories can be used to
guide nursing practice. Research studies which uncover the meaning of
experience can help nurses become more aware of issues important to
diverse populations. Currently, many cities have nurse-managed clinics
operating in their homeless shelters. Many cities still do not. Health
care, mental health care, and health promotion are central issues to
homeless families. Providing on site services to homeless families does
more than save time for families traveling to and from agencies. It
stimulates a feeling of community among the residents. Energy can be
spent looking for jobs, looking for housing or planning an education
instead of searching daily for other necessities, such as health care.
Children can begin to feel secure in a place which truly shelters them
from the deprivation of homelessness. Nurses can develop, fund, staff
and manage health care centers. Additional services can be offered on
site through the health care center as nurses network with other
professionals. Nurses working on site can influence shelter staff in the
areas of building cleanliness, the nutritional content of meals, safe play
areas for children, and the formation of resident support groups. Nurses
can offer parenting classes not only in basic child behavior and
development, but also on issues such as how to advocate for your child
at school, how to talk with your child, and how children exhibit stress.

The most common problem limiting the extent of nurses
involvement in homeless shelters is lack of funding. Nurses need to

become more aware of funding resources. This may involve enlisting local business college students or professors to work jointly with nursing in the development of a business plan which can provide money for needed programs. Community volunteers can be recruited to participate in a shelter day care center, after school programs, or adult literacy programs.

IMPLICATIONS FOR NURSING EDUCATION

Nursing education must provide the links between practice and theory. In the classroom, theory can be used to understand practice issues which will later be confronted in practice settings. Community-based learning must be encouraged as nursing practice moves out of the hospital and into the community.

This study can be used to help students understand the experience of children who are homeless. Additionally, it can be used to stimulate discussions about vulnerable children and societal neglect. Ongoing studies about what is meaningful to children will eventually culminate in theory development.

This study was unique in its approach to understanding children's perspectives. Perhaps this study's most important contribution to nursing science lies in the underlying premise that children have an original worldview which has largely been neglected by research. Their perspective is valuable and accessible to researchers who are willing to adjust traditional research methods to enable children's voices to be heard. Nursing students will benefit from exposure to creative solutions to research and practice problems.

CONCLUSION

Research studies focusing on the strengths of families will foster theory development which in turn will guide program development. The problems are large but not insurmountable. Researchers and professionals do not have to produce the answers, and solve the problems for America's vulnerable families. The goal must be to provide opportunities for individuals and families to find their own truths. In her work as a play therapist, Violet Oaklander describes her goal,

> I must remember that my task is to
> help children feel strong within
> themselves to help them see the world
> as it really is. I want them to know
> that they have choices about how
> they will live in their world, how they
> will react to it, how they will

manipulate it. I cannot presump-
tuously make this choice for them. I
can only do my part to give them the
strength to make those choices they
want to make, and to know when
choices are impossible to make.[30]

As health care professionals, it is vitally important to remember
that people must choose their own paths. Watson's view of
interconnectedness and shared humaneness provides a framework for
dealing with vulnerable families. The nurse's caring concern can help
families heal.

NOTES

1. Heusel, K.J. (1990). "The experience of homelessness viewed through the eyes of homeless school-age children." (Doctoral Dissertation, Ohio State University, 1990). *University Microfilms International.*
2. Hubbard, J. (1991). *Shooting Back, A Photographic View of the Life of Homeless Children.* San Francisco, CA: Chronicle Books.
3. Hubbard, see note 2 above.
4. Konner, M. (1991). *Childhood, A Multicultural View.* Boston, MA: Little Brown and Co.
5. Bassuk, E., & Rubin, L. (1987). "Homeless children: A neglected population." *American Journal of Orthopsychiatry,* 76(9), 1097-1101; Rossi, P.H. (1989). *Down and Out in America.* Chicago: University of Chicago Press; Wright, J.D. (1991). "Children in and of the streets: Health, social policy, and the homeless young." *American Journal of Diseases of Children,* 145, 516-519.
6. Clarke, P., Williams, C., Percy, M., & Kim, Y. (1995). "Health and life problems of homeless men and women in the southeast." *Journal of Community Health Nursing,* 12(2), 101-110.
7. Bassuk & Rubin, see note 5 above; Davidhizar, R., & Frank, B. (1992). "Understanding the physical and psychosocial stressors of the child who is homeless." *Pediatric Nursing,* 18(6), 559-562.
8. Wood, D. (1989). "Homeless children: Their evaluation and treatment." *Journal of Pediatric Health Care,* 3(4), 194-199.
9. Heusel, see note 1 above.
10. Bassuk, E.L., & Gallagher, E.M. (1990). "The impact of homelessness on children." *Child and Youth Services,* 14(1), 19-33.
11. Grey, M. (1990). "Helping children cope with stress." *Journal of Pediatric Health Care,* 4(6), 309-310.
12. Hunter, L. (1993). "Sibling play therapy and homeless children: An opportunity in the crisis." *Child Welfare,* 72(1), 65-74.
13. Dixon, S., & Stern, M. (1992). *Encounters with Children: Pediatric behavior and development.* Boston: Mosby Year Book.
14. Grey, see note 11 above.
15. Bassuk & Gallagher, see note 10 above.
16. Hunter, see note 12 above.
17. Garmezy, N. (1993). "Children in poverty: Resilience despite risk." *Psychiatry Interpersonal and Biological Processes,* 56(1), 127-136.
18. Hunter, see note 12 above; Garmezy, see note 17 above; Bassuk & Gallagher, see note 10 above.
19. Watson, J. (1988). *Nursing: Human Science and Human Care.* New York: National League for Nursing.
20. Watson, see note 19 above.

21. Hunter, see note 12 above.
22. Bassuk & Gallagher, see note 10 above.
23. Dixon & Stein, see note 13 above.
24. Hamburg, D. (1994). *Today's Children, Creating a Future for a Generation in Crisis.* NY: Random House, Inc.
25. Hamburg, see note 24 above.
26. Goodman, L., Saxe, L, & Harvey, M. (1991). "Homelessness as psychological trauma." *American Psychologist*, 46(11), 1219-1225.
27. Goodman, Saxe & Harvey, see note 26 above.
28. Luthar, S.S., & Zigler, E. (1991). "Vulnerability and competence: A review of research on resilience in childhood." *American Journal of Orthopsychiatry*, 61(1), 6-22.
29. Bassuk & Gallagher, see note 10 above.
30. Oaklander, V. (1988). *Windows to Our Children.* Highland, NY: The Gestalt Journal Press.

Appendix

1) Take your pictures out and look at them.
2) How did you decide what pictures to take?
3) Were there too many pictures or could you have taken more?
4) Do the pictures show what you want them to show?
5) Do you like your pictures?
6) Pick the 10 you like the best, and tell us about them?
7) Now pick the 5 that you like the best.
8) Was it easy or hard to pick five?

I will enlarge these 5 special pictures and next time we will talk more about them.

1) Take your pictures out and look at them.
2) Order the 5 pictures from the most special to the least.
3) Tell about each picture, why it is special and why it is in the order you put it in.
4) Take the most special picture, tell it's story. Was it always special, how did it get to be special, what is special about it now that wasn't before?
5) Make a statement about the picture - a title.
6) Is there anything you didn't have a chance to take a picture of that you would have liked to take a picture of?
7) Now take all of the pictures, and sort them into not more than four different groups.
8) What categories did you use and why? Give each category a title.
9) Is there anything else you would like to tell about the pictures?
10) How did you feel about doing this project?

References

Ammerman, R.T., Cassisi, J.E., Hersen, M. & Van Hasselt, V.B. (1986). "Consequences of physical abuse and neglect in children." *Clinical Psychology Review*, 6, 291-310.

Axline, V. (1947). *Play Therapy*. NY, NY: Ballantine Books.

Ball, M.S. & Smith, G.W. (1992). *Analyzing Visual Data*. Newbury Park, CA: Sage Publications.

Bassuk, E.L., & Gallagher, E.M. (1990). "The impact of homelessness on children." *Child and Youth Services*, 14(1), 19-33.

Bassuk, E.L., & Rosenberg, L. (1988). "Why does family homelessness occur? A case-control study." *American Journal of Public Health*, 78(7), 783-788.

Bassuk, E., & Rubin, L. (1987). "Homeless children: A neglected population." *American Journal of Orthopsychiatry*, 57(2), 279-286.

Bassuk, E.L., Rubin, L., & Lauriat, M.A. (1986). "Characteristics of sheltered homeless families." *American Journal of Public Health*, 76(9), 1097-1101.

Baumann, S.L. (1993). "The meaning of being homeless." *Scholarly Inquiry for Nursing Practice: An International Journal*, 7(1), 59-73.

Beach, D. & Sokoloff, M. (1974). "Spatially dominated nonverbal communication of children: A methodological study." *Perceptual and Motor Skills*, 38, 1303-1310.

Beitchman, J.H., Zucker, K.J., Hood, J.E., DaCosta, G.A., Akman, D. & Cassavia, E. (1992). "A review of the long-term effects of child sexual abuse." *Child Abuse and Neglect*, 16, 101-118.

Berck, J. (1992). *No Place To Be: Voices of Homeless Children*. Boston: Houghton Mifflin Company.

Berne, A.S., Dato, C., Mason, D.J., & Rafferty, M. (1990). "A nursing model for addressing the health needs of homeless families." *Image*, 22(1), 8-13.

Bernthal, N. L. (1990). "Motherhood lost and found: The experience of becoming an adoptive mother to a foreign-born child." (Doctoral dissertation, The Union). *University Microfilms International*.

Blount, K. (1992). "Chronic Psychological Manifestations." In S. Ludwig & A. Kornberg (Eds.), *Child Abuse a Medical Reference*. NY, NY: Churchill Livingstone.

Case, C. & Dalley, T. (1992). *The Handbook of Art Therapy*. New York: Routledge.

Clarke, P., Williams, C., Percy, M., & Kim, Y. (1995). "Health and life problems of homeless men and women in the southeast." *Journal of Community Health Nursing*, 12(2), 101-110.

Collier, J. & Collier, M. (1986). *Visual Anthropology: Photography as a Research Method.* Albuquerque, NM; University of New Mexico Press.

Davidhizar, R., & Frank, B. (1992). "Understanding the physical and psychosocial stressors of the child who is homeless." *Pediatric Nursing*, 18(6), 559-562.

Deatrick, J. & Faux, S. (1991). "Conducting qualitative studies with children and adolescents." In J.M. Morse (Ed.) *Qualitative Nursing Research.* Newbury Park, CA: Sage.

Delpo, E.G. & Frick, S. (1988). "Directed and nondirected play as therapeutic modalities." *Children's Health Care: Journal of the Association for the Care of Children's Health*, 16, 261-267.

Denehy, J.A. (1990). "Communicating with children through drawings." In M.J. Craft & J.A. Denehy (Eds.) *Nursing Interventions for Infants and Children.* Phila., PA: W.B. Saunders Co.

Denzin, N.K. (1989). *The Research Act.* Englewood Cliffs, NJ: Prentice-Hall.

Dixon, S. & Stern, M. (1992). *Encounters with Children: Pediatric Behavior and Development.* Boston: Mosby Year Book.

Douglass, B.G., & Moustakas, C. (1985). "Heuristic inquiry: The internal search to know." *Journal of Humanistic Psychology*, 25(3), 39-55.

Eth, S. & Pynoos, R.S. (1985). *Post-traumatic Stress Disorder in Children.* Washington, DC: American Psychiatric Press, Inc.

Faux, S.A., Walsh, M., Deatrick, J.A. (1988). "Intensive interviewing of children and adolescents." *Western Journal of Nursing Research*, 10(2), 180-193.

Foscarinis, M. (1991). "The politics of homelessness." *American Psychologist*, 46(11), 1232-1238.

Garmezy, N. (1993). "Children in poverty: Resilience despite risk." *Psychiatry Interpersonal and Biological Processes*, 56(1), 127-136.

Gillis, C., Highley, B., Roberts, B., & Martinson, I. (1989). *Toward a Science of Family Nursing.* Menlo Park, CA: Addison Wesley Publishing Company.

Gladding, S. (1993, July). "Poetry and creative writing." In P. Paisley (Ed.), *Expressive Arts and Play Media in Counseling.* Symposium conducted at Appalachian State University, Boone, North Carolina.

Green, A.H. (1985). "Children traumatized by physical abuse." In S. Eth & R.S. Pynoos (Eds.), *Post-traumatic Stress Disorder in Children.* Washington, DC: American Psychiatric Press, Inc.

Grey, M. (1990). "Helping children cope with stress." *Journal of Pediatric Health Care*, 4(6), 309-310.

Goodman, L., Saxe, L., & Harvey, M. (1991). "Homelessness as psychological trauma." *American Psychologist*, 46(11), 1219-1225.

Grigsby, C., Baumann, D., Gregorich, S.E. & Roberts-Gray, C. (1990). "Disaffiliation to entrenchment: A model for understanding homelessness." *Journal of Social Issues*, 46(4), 141-156.

Guba, E. (1990). *The Paradigm Dialog*. Newbury Park, CA: Sage Publications, Inc.

Guerney, L.F. (1983). "Client-centered (nondirective) play therapy." In C. Schaefer & K. O'Connor (Eds.) *Handbook of Play Therapy*. NY: John Wiley & Sons.

Haase, J.E. & Myers, S.T. (1988). "Reconciling paradigm assumptions of qualitative and quantitative research." *Western Journal of Nursing Research*, 10(2), 128-137.

Hamburg, D. (1994). *Today's Children, Creating a Future for a Generation in Crisis*. NY: Random House, Inc.

Heusel, K.J. (1990). "The experience of homelessness viewed through the eyes of homeless school-age children" (Doctoral dissertation, Ohio State University, 1990). *University Microfilms International*.

Hogan, P.T. (1981). "Phototherapy in the educational setting." *The Arts in Psychotherapy*, 8, 193-199.

Hubbard, J. (1991). *Shooting Back, A Photographic View of Life of Homeless Children*. San Francisco, CA: Chronicle Books.

Humphreys, J. (1991). "Children of battered women: Worries about their mothers." *Pediatric Nursing*, 17(4), 342-346.

Hunter, L. (1993). "Sibling play therapy with homeless children: An opportunity in the crisis." *Child Welfare*, 72(1), 65-74.

Issel, L., Ersek, M. & Lewis, F. (1990). "How children cope with mother's breast cancer." *Oncology Nursing Forum*, 17(3), 5-13.

Konner, M. (1991). *Childhood, A Multicultural View*. Boston, MA: Little, Brown and Co.

Kramer, E. (1977). "Art therapy and play." *American Journal of Art Therapy*, 17, 3-11.

Kozol, J. (1988). *Rachel and Her Children: Homeless Families in America*. NY: Fawcett Columbine.

Landreth, G. (1991). *Play Therapy: The Art of the Relationship*. Munice, IN: Accelerated Development Inc. Publishers.

Luthar, S.S., & Zigler, E. (1991). "Vulnerability and competence: A review of research on resilience in childhood." *American Journal of Orthopsychiatry*, 61(1), 6-22.

Malchiodi, C. (1990). *Breaking the Silence, Art Therapy With Children From Violent Homes*. NY, NY: Bruner/Mazel Publishers.

Mayeroff, M. (1972). *On Caring*. NY, NY: Harper Collins Publishing.

Manicus & Secord cited in Rogers, C. (1989). "A human science." In H. Kirschenbaum & V.L. Henderson(Eds.), *The Carl Rogers Reader*. Boston: Houghton Mifflin Company.

Marshall, C. (1990). "Goodness criteria: Are they objective or judgement calls?" In E.G. Guba (Ed.), *The Paradigm Dialog*. CA: Sage Publications, Inc.

Molnar, J., Rath, W., & Klein, T. (1990). "Constantly compromised: The impact of homelessness on children." *Journal of Social Issues*, 46(4), 109-123.

Moustakas, C. (1961). *Loneliness*. Englewood Cliffs, NY: Prentice-Hall.

Moustakas, C. (1990). *Heuristic Research*. Newbury Park, CA: Sage Publications.

Murata, J., Mace, J.P., Strehlow, A., & Shuler, P.(1992). "Disease patterns in homeless children: A comparison with national data." *Journal of Pediatric Nursing*, 7(3), 196-203.

Nickerson, E. (1983). "Art as a play therapeutic medium." In C.E. Schaefer & K.J. O'Connor (Eds.), *Handbook of Play Therapy*. New York: John Wiley & Sons.

Oaklander, V. (1988). *Windows to Our Children*. Highland, NY: The Gestalt Journal Press.

Parker, R.M., Rescorla, L.A., Finkelstein, J.A., Barnes, N., Holmes, J.H., & Stolley, P.D. (1991). "A survey of the health of homeless children in Philadelphia shelters." *American Journal of Diseases of Children*, 145, 520-526.

Parse, R.R. (1987). *Nursing Science*. Phila., PA: W.B. Saunders Company.

Patton, M.Q. (1980). *Qualitative Evaluation and Research Methods*. Newbury Park, CA: Sage Publications.

Rafferty, Y. & Shinn, M. (1991). "The impact of homelessness on children." *American Psychologist*, 46(11), 1170-1179.

Rescorla, L., Parker, R., & Stolley, P. (1991). "Ability, achievement, and adjustment in homeless children." *American Journal of Orthopsychiatry*, 61(2), 210-220.

Rogers, C. (1961). *On Becoming a Person*. Boston, MA:Houghton Mifflin Company.

Rossi, P. H. (1989). *Down and Out in America*. Chicago: University of Chicago Press.

Rossi, P.H., Wright, J., Fisher, G., & Willis, G. (1987). "The urban homeless: Estimating composition and size." *Science*, 235, 1336-1341.

Roth, E. A. & Barrett, R.P. (1980). "Parallels in art and play therapy with a disturbed retarded child." *The Arts In Psychotherapy*, 7, 19-26.

Ryan, N. (1989). "Stress-coping strategies identified from school age children's perspective." *Research in Nursing and Health*, 111-122.

Satir, V. (1983). *Conjoint Family Therapy*. Palo Alto, CA: Science and Behavior Books.

Stern, J., & Urdang, L. (Eds.). (1973). *The Random House Dictionary of the English Language*. NY: Random House

Shinn, M., Knickman, J.R., & Weitzman, B.C. (1991). "Social relationships and vulnerability to becoming homeless among poor families." *American Psychologist*, 46(11), 1180-1187.

Schulsinger, E. (1990). "Needs of sheltered homeless children." *Journal of Pediatric Health Care*, 4(3), 136-140.

Snyder, R. (1988). "The experience of rejecting love." (Doctoral Dissertation, The Union). *University Microfilms International.*

Talento, B. (1990). "Jean Watson." In J. George (Ed.), *Nursing Theories: The Base for Professional Nursing Practice*. Norwalk, CN: Appleton & Lange.

Thomas, G.V. & Silk, A. (1990). *An Introduction to the Psychology of Children's Drawings*. NY, NY: New York University Press.

Wadeson, H. (1978). "Art therapy data in research." *American Journal of Art Therapy*, 18, 11-18.

Watson, J. (1987). "Academic and clinical collaboration: Advancing the art and science of human caring." *Communicating Nursing Research, Vol. 20, Collaboration in Nursing Research: Advancing the Science of Human Care*. Western Institute of Nursing. Proceedings of the Western Society for Research in Nursing Conference, Tempe, AZ, April/May.

Watson, J. (1988). *Nursing: Human Science and Human Care*. New York: National League for Nursing.

Watson, J. (1989). "Human caring and suffering: A Subjective model for health sciences." In R. Taylor & J. Watson (Eds.) *They Shall Not Hurt, Human Suffering and Human Caring*. Boulder, CO: Colorado Associated University Press.

Whitman, B.Y., Accardo, P., Boyert, M., & Kendagor, R. (1990). "Homelessness and cognitive performance in children: A possible link." *Social Work*, 35(6), 516-519.

Wolf, R. (1976). "The polaroid technique: Spontaneous dialogues from the unconscious." *Art Psychotherapy*, 3, 197-214.

Wood, D. (1989). "Homeless children: Their evaluation and treatment." *Journal of Pediatric Health Care*, 3(4),194-199.

Wood, D (1992). "Evaluation and management of homeless families and children." In D. Wood (Ed.), *Delivering Health Care to Homeless Persons*. NY, NY: Springer Publishing.

Wright, J.D. (1991). "Children in and of the streets: Health, social policy, and the homeless young." *American Journal of Diseases of Children*, 145, 516- 519.

Zwick, D. (1978). "Photography as a tool toward increased awareness of the aging self." *Art Psychotherapy*, 5,135-141.

Index

Reagan/Bush Administration, 3
relieving stress, 66
resiliency, 38
resilient, 77
Rogers, C. 8
schools, 4
separate, 27
separation, 79
shelter, 15, 41,44, 52, 56, 61,
   65, 67, 69, 76
siblings, 68
sister, 58
social disaffiliation, 16

social supports, 16
special, 6, 19, 23, 39, 43, 80
stressful, 19
survival, 26
themes, 25, 65, 80
trauma, 5
truancy, 4
trust, 67, 79
trustworthiness, 44
unemployment, 4
understood., 25
violence, 3, 16
Watson, J. 7, 10, 35, 78, 83